JESSE JAMES
AND THE
LOST
TEMPLAR
TREASURE

"Daniel J. Duke has successfully cracked open part of the mystery surrounding Templar treasure from Jerusalem that had been moved to the Americas to help establish a free nation. *Jesse James and the Lost Templar Treasure* goes beyond just theorizing that treasure was moved to the Americas and in fact demonstrates the connections and methods utilized to hide certain treasures. There have always been those who have sought to shape history to ensure that freedoms and artifacts could be preserved in the Americas. Daniel J. Duke's book is on the cutting edge of revealing some of what has remained hidden. Anybody who is interested in the Templar legacy and their connection with the Americas will find true gems in this book!"

TIMOTHY W. HOGAN, TEMPLAR GRAND MASTER,
AUTHOR, AND LECTURER

"Having inadvertently fallen down one of the many hidden wells of esoteric knowledge dotted across the North American landscape, author Daniel J. Duke—the great-great-grandson of the outlaw Jesse James—weaves a wonderful tale of Southern intrigue and mysterious treasure. His familial connection enables him to explore the ancient mysteries within the Tree of Life and Veil templates and their connections over time to the Freemasons, the

Knights Templar, the Knights of the Golden Circle, Francis Bacon and the Rosicrucians, and Sovereign Grand Commander Albert Pike. Where he travels next on his personal journey of discovery will be the key."

WILLIAM F. MANN, AUTHOR OF
THE KNIGHTS TEMPLAR IN THE NEW WORLD,
THE TEMPLAR MERIDIANS, AND
TEMPLAR SANCTUARIES IN NORTH AMERICA

JESSE JAMES
AND THE
LOST
TEMPLAR
TREASURE

SECRET DIARIES,
CODED MAPS, AND THE
KNIGHTS OF THE GOLDEN CIRCLE

DANIEL J. DUKE

Destiny Books
Rochester, Vermont

Destiny Books
One Park Street
Rochester, Vermont 05767
www.DestinyBooks.com

Destiny Books is a division of Inner Traditions International

Cataloging-in-Publication Data for this title is available from the Library of Congress

ISBN 978-1-62055-820-1 (print)
ISBN 978-1-62055-821-8 (ebook)

Printed and bound in the United States

10   9   8   7   6   5   4   3   2

Text design by Debbie Glogover and layout by Virginia Scott Bowman
This book was typeset in Garamond Premier Pro with S&S Amberosa and
Gill Sans MT Pro used as display fonts

To send correspondence to the author of this book, mail a first-class letter to the
author c/o Inner Traditions • Bear & Company, One Park Street, Rochester, VT
05767, and we will forward the communication.

For my late mother, mentor,
and favorite author, Betty Dorsett Duke.

ACKNOWLEDGMENTS

I thank God and my mother for all of their assistance. I would like to express my most profound gratitude to my literary agent, Fiona Spencer Thomas. I also thank my sister, Teresa Duke, my father, Joe Duke, and my brother, John Duke, for the help and tremendous support they have provided. Much appreciation and thanks to my friend author Philippa Lee (Faulks) for her invaluable assistance. I would also like to express my profound gratitude to my editor, Kayla Toher, for the invaluable help and advice.

CONTENTS

He, that concealed things will find,
must look before him, and behind.

GEORGE WITHER, *A COLLECTION OF*
EMBLEMS ANCIENT AND MODERN

Everyone is free to reject and dissent from whatsoever
herein may seem to him to be untrue or unsound. It is
only required of him that he shall weigh what is taught,
and give it a fair hearing and unprejudiced judgement.

ALBERT PIKE, *MORALS AND DOGMA OF*
THE ANCIENT AND ACCEPTED SCOTTISH
RITE OF FREEMASONRY

THE HUNT FOR TRUTH AND TREASURE

You, dear reader, are invited to come along with me on one of the greatest treasure hunts in American history, if not the world. Treasures that took centuries to amass and at least that long to hide. Treasures made up not just of gold, silver, and gems but also of knowledge. When we are done, you may decide these treasures are best left where they are for now, and you can walk away with a wealth of knowledge and the satisfaction that you know who was involved, what they hid, and why something like this had to remain hidden for so long.

The entire journey leading me to this point has been an exciting one, and I believe this is an appropriate place to give you a little background into how I stumbled onto this story. In 1995, I was in Houston, Texas, just out of college and working for an engineering company. My mother, Betty Dorsett Duke, called me at the office and told me she had some news. As she told me, my memory of all the stories I had heard growing up came to mind. I could tell Mom was excited, and when she finished telling her news, I was excited too.

Jesse James was our ancestor. The outlaw Jesse James. Mom, my sister, Teresa, and I thought the world would be excited as well, not because Jesse was our ancestor, but because he did not die as history

1

had stated. "America's Robin Hood" faked his death in 1882 and lived the remainder of his long life in Blevins, Texas, under the alias of James Lafayette Courtney. Mom contacted the James Farm and Museum in Kearney, Missouri, and much to our surprise, they were not happy at all; in fact, they were quite rude about our discovery, and that experience would be the first of many rude encounters.

We—my mother, sister, and I—continued the research. Instead of relying just on our word and on family stories, my mother took our family photos to the experts. By experts, I don't mean someone who paints for a hobby or has read a few books about photo identification. Mom went to the forensics lab of the Texas Department of Public Safety, the forensic photographic expert for the Austin Police Department, and a company called Visionics (world leaders in facial recognition technology, later purchased by Identix). All three verified that our family photographs and tintypes of my great-great-grandfather, who lived under the alias of James Lafayette Courtney, matched the image of the famous (or infamous) outlaw Jesse James. Not only did the photos of our ancestor match the historically accepted photos of Jesse James, but photos of his mother matched Jesse's mother, down to the very dress she wore. Other family photos matched those of Jesse's family as well.

Combing through my great-great-grandfather's diary revealed even more about him. Not only did he list known James Gang members, but he even signed the entries by his name, Jesse James. Census records, birth certificates, marriage certificates, and other official documents, combined with newspaper articles and history books, just added to our findings.

The James Farm and Museum and some of those connected to it claimed they had DNA proving that Jesse died as history stated. My mother disproved that claim as well. She shot their story down, and did it in as polite and professional a manner as a person could, proving that the 1995 exhumation of the alleged grave of Jesse James, upon which they placed so much confidence, was a farce. Stephen Caruso, the deputy counselor for Clay County, Missouri, at the time of the 1995 exhumation and DNA testing of the reported grave of Jesse James, told the *Kearney Courier* the whole thing was "phony." "They [the James Farm and Museum] tried to do DNA testing on remains that weren't Jesse James," Caruso said. He claimed that someone lost Jesse's hair that was to be tested, but then it suddenly turned up. He also claimed that someone submitted their own hair in place of the lost hair. He told me and my mother, in his office, who that someone was and exactly how and why it was done.

Shortly after Mom had proven the DNA findings to be false, the rude behavior turned into harassment and even death threats, which were quickly taken care of, with many thanks to the FBI. My mother knew she was right, and she was not going to stop. She never did stop. She was honest, professional, and courteous and lived by an old Texas Ranger quote she loved: "No man (or woman) in the wrong can stand up against a fellow (or lady) that's in the right and keeps on a-comin.'" Sadly, on August 29, 2015, our mother passed away. She never gave up and she always fought for the truth. She taught us to do the same. She had proven with photos and records that Jesse James did not die as history states, but rather faked his death in 1882 and lived the remainder of his life in Texas under the alias of James Lafayette Courtney. My sister, Teresa, and I are honored to follow in her footsteps, and we fully intend to follow through with what our mother started.

In addition to leaving behind diaries, letters, and photographs, Jesse also left a few maps leading to treasures. With a map in hand, it seems that things should be easy from the start, but like everything involving Jesse James, nothing is ever what it seems on the surface. He was an intelligent and complex man, and locating the treasures he buried would prove to be very difficult. But like my mother, I love solving a great mystery.

1 KNIGHTS, OUTLAWS, AND TREASURE MAPS

After my mother wrote her first book, titled *Jesse James Lived and Died in Texas,* published in 1998, she, my sister, Teresa, and I continued our research. I had more time then to focus on the coded messages Jesse had written on his treasure map and in the diary he left behind. The codes did not seem very complicated, but the locations of the treasures the maps lead to were never given. Nevertheless, I had a few good leads due to family stories passed down through the generations.

Jesse was known to have hidden cash, gold, and silver around his home in Blevins, Texas. After he passed away in 1943, one of his sons lost the property. The new owner was said to have found money in the walls of the house and in various locations around the property. This information was relayed to my mother by one of the new owner's relatives. I was curious about it, so I checked out the county tax records and noticed that around the time some of the smaller treasure caches were said to have been found, the son of the new owner had begun to purchase large tracts of farmland around the area. Coincidence? Maybe. After the new owner passed away, his son took over the property, and he doesn't let anyone enter.

Fig. 1.1. Jesse Woodson James aka James L. Courtney

It's well known among Jesse James researchers and many Civil War historians that Jesse, like many young men in western Missouri, joined a group of pro-Confederate guerillas, commonly referred to as Quantrill's Partisan Rangers. He did this after he and his family suffered a brutal attack by pro-Union guerrillas known as Red Legs. The actions of the guerillas were not approved on Union authority; many Missourians supported the Union side even though theirs was a slave state. The Younger brothers, who later became well-known James Gang members, were from a family of Union supporters, until a group of Jayhawkers, Union-supporting guerillas, robbed and murdered their father. Incidents like this pitted neighbor against neighbor and led many young men to join guerilla forces to protect their family or seek retribution for harms committed. Jesse was strapped to a plow and severely beaten, his pregnant mother was pushed around, and his stepfather was hanged by a rope and suffered permanent brain damage from the ordeal. Jesse wanted revenge. He was too young to enlist in the regular Confederate forces, but he found a group that was willing to let him fight, even at the young age of fourteen. While there is no proof, this is when Jesse is said to have been initiated into a pro-Southern group known as the Knights of the Golden Circle (KGC).

Jesse James's outlaw years were an unfortunate result of the Civil War. One could make a very strong argument that Jesse and the men who rode with him weren't left many (or any) options when the war was over. They were hunted like animals, and often, those who were caught or surrendered were executed. Some question why Jesse and the men he rode with did not just turn themselves in after the Civil War ended, like all the other soldiers. The answer to that is easy. The guerillas weren't granted amnesty like all the other soldiers.

Jesse's family lived in Missouri during the Civil War. Missouri, a slave state under the Missouri Compromise, sat on the border between the North and the South. Because of its location, many families did not agree with the state's designation, and the war became especially personal. Some citizens fought for the Union side, so attacks on Union sympathizers by Confederate guerillas, or attacks from the Union side on Confederate supporters, were essentially attacks on one's neighbors. This is why guerilla fighters, who committed acts not formally sanctioned by war, were not granted amnesty as Confederate soldiers were. But if your family had been brutally attacked, with no one around to help you and no other recourse than fight or flight, what would you do? Would you stay and defend yourself, your family, and your property, or would you flee? Would you fight, or would you take the risk of dying on the road in an ambush and losing everything you and your family had ever worked for? It's a hard question to answer, but they made their choice, stood behind it, and paid the price. Had they fled, the price may have been much more severe.

Jesse, like so many others in the past, came to Texas several years after the close of the war for a new start in life. When he came to Texas, he changed his identity to James Lafayette Courtney. He began to wind down his illegal activities, and after 1882, he lived the remainder of his life as an upstanding citizen leading a law-abiding, productive life under his assumed name. He also became a Freemason. Jesse, under the name of James L. Courtney, belonged to the Carolina Lodge, No. 330, in Lott, Texas, until 1884, when he moved to the Mooreville Lodge, No. 639, which was closer to his home in Blevins.

What about the Knights of the Golden Circle, to which he allegedly belonged? This was "a secretive organization created in 1854, proposed to establish a slaveholding empire encompassing the southern United States, the West Indies, Mexico, and parts of Central America. Centering on Havana, this empire would be some 2,400 miles in diameter—hence the name Golden Circle."[1] George W. L. Bickley, a Virginia-born doctor, editor, and adventurer, was one of the founders.

According to the records of the KGC convention held in 1860, the organization was founded in Kentucky in 1854, but isn't said to have become "active" until sometime between 1859 and 1860. "Many prominent Texans joined the K.G.C., and Bickley even courted Gov. Sam Houston who reportedly became an initiate. Houston, however, regardless of his interest in annexing Mexico to the United States, could not accept the K.G.C.'s anti-Union stance and refused to support its schemes."[2] After the Civil War had ended, one of the KGC's goals is said to have included raising enough money to fund a second war, which, we all know, never happened.

There are claims that the famous Freemason and former Confederate brigadier general Albert Pike was a member of the KGC. Again, I have yet to see any proof that Albert Pike, or Jesse James for that matter, were members. I wouldn't think it unlikely that they were, but without proof, any such claims are purely speculation. Jesse James and the men he rode with during the Civil War were branded outlaws and denied amnesty. They were left with very few choices: they could turn themselves in and face the hangman's noose, try to hide, or live up to their new brand and turn to outlawry. After they were branded as outlaws, it's easy for researchers to connect them with any group that fits. Jesse James and Albert Pike fought with the South, and the KGC was a pro-Southern organization, so many have lumped them in with that organization without having any real proof.

What is known is that the KGC was active before and during the Civil War. After the war ended, they are said by some to have disbanded, while others claim they went underground. They were highly secretive, and anyone can say anything about a group like that without being proven right or wrong, because there is little to no evidence to prove otherwise. It does stand to reason, though, that after all the time and effort they spent in attempting to realize their goals, at least some of the members of the KGC would have refused to just walk away.

Among the treasures said to have been buried by the KGC are caches containing weapons, clothing, and other supplies, as well as gold, silver, cash, and other items of value that were said to have been guarded. These caches of treasure are said to range in size from small jars with a few coins to large underground vaults allegedly worth millions of dollars. They are said to be buried all over the country as well as in Mexico and Canada. Some even claim there are caches as far south as Brazil, where many Southern families, known as Confederados, relocated before and during the Civil War.[3]

While trying to identify the location of Jesse's treasure map and researching the KGC for any clues, I came across something known as a KGC treasure template. Supposedly, the KGC would bury their treasures using a template so that others in the know would be able to find them and could make a withdrawal or deposit if and when it was necessary. This makes sense, as it is more logical than digging random holes in the ground.

In the treasure template on page 9, the five squares located in the center and in each of the four corners are supposed to be where the largest treasure caches are located. The stars and circles or dots are said by some to mark the locations of smaller caches. As for the eight symbols that many refer to as "turkey tracks," I have heard several theories. Some say each turkey track represents the location of three or even four caches. Others say they are the locations of landmarks denoting what direction should be followed. Some treasure hunters claim that this is only part of the template and that you need the other half, which works

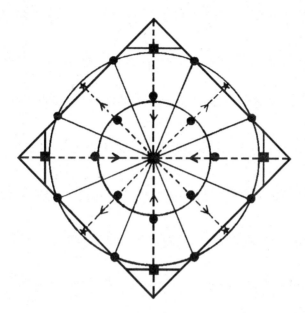

Fig. 1.2. Alleged KGC treasure template

as an overlay; only then will you get a precise location of the treasure caches in an area.

Where did the template come from? One clue leading to an answer to that question is best told by my mother in her second book, *The Truth About Jesse James,* in which she writes:

Dalton [J. Frank Dalton] arrived in Marble Falls, [Texas,] just months after my great-grandfather (Jesse James aka James L. Courtney) died on April 14, 1943. Was his main purpose for being there to learn all he could about Jesse James from my grandmother? All of this occurred before September 5, 1948, the date Dalton publicly proclaimed to be the original Jesse James.

Another incident involving my grandmother and Dalton happened in the late 1940s. My uncle Howard "Boy" Dorsett told his son Bill Dorsett that he visited an old member of the James Gang in Brackenridge Hospital in Austin, Texas during the late 1940s. Uncle Boy is now deceased but his wife, Violet McCracken Dorsett, confirmed this story. They said that my grandmother, who was also Bill's grandmother, read about an old James Gang member being in Brackenridge Hospital and went to see him. She took along a picture of her father and showed the old outlaw who looked at it and said, "That's the Real Jesse James."[4]

When asked what the old outlaw's name was, no one could remember, but my mother found her answer while perusing newspaper articles at the Center for American History in Austin, Texas. The following article caught her eye: "In Local Hospital, 'Jesse James' Scoffs at Treasure Hunters." It said, "A white-bearded old man who claims to be the real Jesse James said Sunday the Zanesville, Ohio treasure hunters are wasting their time. 'They aren't going to find it. It wasn't put there to find,' 101-year-old Frank Dalton hooted. J. Frank Dalton was under an oxygen tent at Brackenridge Hospital Sunday being treated for pneumonia."[5]

My mother also wrote that "some Knights of the Golden Circle treasure hunters use treasure maps drawn by Orvus Lee Howk/Hawk per Dalton's instruction. I have asked if Dalton ever mentioned buried treasure until he pretended to be Jesse James, but no one seems to know."[6] After further research and consideration, she concluded, "I think he learned of some treasure sites from my grandmother. Two of the Confederate depositories that are credited to Dalton may be linked to my family story, however, further research is required to either confirm or discredit this theory. Did he get treasure maps from my grandmother? He later claimed that his treasure maps were stolen."[7]

When I got my hands on a copy of the template, I was excited not only for the purpose of locating the treasure, but also because of the possibility that my great-great-grandfather had used a template just like this. There were, however, a couple of problems I had to address: First, I did not know the scale to be used, and, second, I only had one map, and I was not sure of the location. There must be a location and scale for something like this to work. Obviously, I would need at least two known cache locations in order to be able to determine the scale so I could use this template correctly.

In searching for any known treasure discoveries, I quickly found that when researching treasures there are mountains of information, and very little of it is useful for anything other than an entertaining campfire tale. However, there are a few finds out there that are no less than amazing. The treasure hoard of Victorio Peak is one such find, and I hoped that it could help answer my KGC template questions.

2 SEVEN CITIES OF GOLD

In 1937, a man by the name of Milton Ernest "Doc" Noss was hunting in the Hembrillo Basin area of New Mexico. He is said to have climbed a small rock outcropping less than 500 feet high and sat down, scanning the area for a deer to shoot. When he sat down, he noticed air coming from a hole beneath the rock he was sitting on. He moved the rock and found the entrance to a cave that is said to have held treasure worth over $3 billion.

While exploring the cave, Doc is said to have found chests full of coins and jewels, saddle bags, over 16,000 bars of gold weighing over 40 pounds each, Wells Fargo boxes, and letters, the most recent dated 1880. According to Kathy Weiser, writing on the Legends of America website, Doc and his wife, Ova "Babe" Noss, "spent every free moment exploring the tunnels inside the mountain, living in a tent at the base of the peak. On each trip, Doc would retrieve two gold bars and as many artifacts as he could carry. At one time, he brought out a crown, which contained two hundred forty-three diamonds and one pigeon-blood ruby. . . . Among the artifacts, Doc is reported to have retrieved were documents dated 1797, which he buried in a Wells Fargo chest along with various other treasures. Although the originals have never been recovered, a copy of one of the documents proved to be a translation from Pope Pius III."[1] In addition to all the treasures mentioned above, Doc is also said to have found numerous swords and twenty-seven skeletons. Some of the skeletons were still bound and tied to the floor inside the tunnel-cavern complex.

Most accounts of this story agree that in 1939, in efforts to expand the narrow passageways of the cavern, Doc made a terrible mistake. He used dynamite, and in doing so collapsed his only known way into the cavern. It's said that he buried much of the gold he recovered in various places around the desert and that because gold was illegal for civilians to own at the time, he tried to make contacts with dealers in the black market. It is also said he became increasingly paranoid and trusted no one. He left his wife, married another woman, drank more, and in 1949, he was shot in the back of the head by one of his business partners.

Doc's former wife, Ova Noss, never gave up trying to recover the treasure from Victorio Peak, but her efforts were greatly hampered when the government decided to extend the boundaries of the White Sands Missile Range in 1955.

An article from the *Los Angeles Times* reports that "in 1958, four airmen from nearby Holloman Air Force Base, including Thomas Berlett, spent several months excavating at the site and claim they discovered stacks of gold bars in several caverns. They took nothing, and tried to get permission to recover the treasure."[2]

The four airmen are said to have passed polygraph tests given to them in the early 1960s by the Air Force and the Secret Service. They were given permission to return to Victorio Peak but claimed they couldn't find their way back into the caverns, because they had dynamited the entrance to prevent others from gaining access. They were later ordered to keep away from the site. People claimed the Army had gone in and removed the treasure; while the Army had admitted to being there, they denied finding any treasure.

While I don't doubt most of the Noss story or the account of the four airmen, parts of the story raise some big questions. Victorio Peak's namesake, for example. It gets its name from Chief Victorio, an Apache chief, who, some historians claim, placed the treasure deep inside the

Fig. 2.1. Victorio Peak, New Mexico

mountain. He is said to have obtained the treasure from robbing and pillaging. But 16,000 bars of gold weighing over 40 pounds each? Approximately 320 tons of gold from robbing and pillaging in the American Southwest? That seems highly unlikely.

To put 320 tons of gold into perspective, let's compare the amount of gold the Spanish acquired from the New World to the 320 tons of gold allegedly stashed inside Victorio Peak by Chief Victorio. "Between 1500 and 1650 the Spanish shipped from America to Europe about 181 tons of gold and 16,000 tons of silver."[3] I seriously doubt that one man and his band of warriors could rob almost twice as much gold in less than 30 years than armies from Spain did in 150 years.

That said, I also doubt that this was a KGC treasure. If the KGC had known about the treasure in Victorio Peak, and if their goal was to fund a second Civil War, then it only makes sense that they would have seized the opportunity to use the funds from Victorio Peak and gone to war. Precious metals are weighted according to a unit of measure referred to as troy weights, which are said to have origi-nated in Troyes, France, during the Middle Ages. One troy pound of gold is equal to 14.5833 ounces instead of 16 ounces. In terms of tons, it depends on whether we're dealing with short, long, or metric tons. In trying to keep this simple, I'll just go with a short ton, which weighs less than the long and metric tons. Three hundred and twenty short tons of gold at approximately 29,166 ounces per ton, priced in 1863 at $30 per ounce, would bring the treasure to a value of around $279 million. Having other large treasures hidden away, the KGC would have had more than enough gold to feed, clothe, and arm a sizeable force for several years.

Then there's the letter Doc Noss is said to have reburied in a Wells Fargo chest. The letter was dated 1797, with a translation from a text by Pope Pius III. That too throws doubt on this being a KGC treasure. The translation from Pope Pius III, who held the papacy for an extremely brief period from September 22, 1503 until October 18, 1503, states the following: "Seven is the Holy number," the passage begins. It then continues for several lines before ending with a cryptic message. "In seven languages, seven signs, and languages in seven foreign nations, look for the Seven Cities of Gold. Seventy miles north of El Paso del Norte in the seventh peak, Soledad, these cities have seven sealed doors, three sealed toward the rising of the Sol sun, three sealed toward the setting of the Sol sun, one deep within Casa del Cueva de Oro, at high noon. Receive health, wealth, and honor."[4] Soledad is said to have been the former name of the peak known as Victorio Peak, and Casa del Cueva de Oro is Spanish for house of the golden cave. If that is true, then it sounds as if Doc Noss stumbled upon at least part of the treasure of Cibola.

That brings up another issue. Researching the legend of Cibola, the Seven Cities of Gold, it is claimed that the legend began with a slave by the name of Estebanico (also spelled Estevanico) who was a part of the Narváez Expedition, which began in 1527. While the expedition was in what is now Texas, they were given a baby rattle made of copper and were told stories of wealthy cities to the north. After the expedition ended, Spanish Viceroy Antonio de Mendoza "dispatched the Franciscan Monk Marcos de Niza to investigate," according to an article on the Ancient History Encyclopedia website, which continues:

Nizas' guide was this Estebanico: Being a survivor of the previous expedition he was believed to be knowledgeable about the lay of the land. Described as a "Black Muslim from Azamoor" (a coastal city in northwestern Morocco), he was an intelligent, educated man and most likely spoke several languages.

In his diary, Friar di Niza noted his disgust of Estebanico by stating he had acquired, "great stores of turquoise and other wealth, as well as many native women." Despondent and angry, Estebanico originally stayed well ahead of the group but as his relationship with Friar di Niza worsened, he stayed so far ahead of the main party their only communication was by a message tied to a cross. It was on one of these messages that Estebanico said he had heard of seven great cities to the north. The people were very wealthy, he wrote, with multi-storey [sic] buildings and fine cotton clothes. Estebanico called these cities Cibola. This was the last message they received from Estebanico as a short time later, the party were told he met the Zuni Indians and they killed him.[5]

The Narváez Expedition started in 1527, and Estebanico was said to have been killed in 1539. Pope Pius III died in 1503, thirty-six years before the legend of Cibola is said to have begun. Either the story of the letter dated 1797 and containing the translation of Pope Pius III is a hoax or the story regarding the beginnings of the legend of Cibola is wrong. Digging deeper, I found what is said by some to be the origins of the legend of Cibola.

The origins of the legend of Cibola began when the Moors invaded Porto, Spain, in the eighth century. Seven bishops in the city gathered all the wealth and fled westward to the Atlantic, to an island called Antilla. When the New World was discovered, many believed they had found Antilla. Bishops, being a part of the church, would have very likely sent word of their departure to others, and this could explain how Pope Pius III came to know about it.

Based on the information I had read, I doubted the treasure was placed there by Chief Victorio or the Knights of the Golden Circle. The Spanish explorers allegedly did not know about it until they heard tales from the native peoples, yet Pope Pius III is said to have written about it sometime before his death in 1503; if so, he may have known of this because of the seven bishops who fled Spain in the eighth century. There are just too many unanswered questions regarding this treasure and whom it belonged to. We know the airmen passed their polygraph tests, and that backs up the stories and witness accounts of the treasures found by Doc Noss, so the evidence that a treasure was found appears to be sound. What doesn't add up are the theories of where the treasure came from. There are other theories as well; like those mentioned above, they left me with more questions than answers.

The lure of the treasure in Victorio Peak is so great that mention of it even appeared in the Watergate hearings in 1973: "John Dean, the former lawyer for President Richard M. Nixon, mentioned that Attorney General John Mitchell had been asked to pull strings to allow some searchers to look for the gold."[6] Former New Mexico Attorney General David Norvell summed it up well when he stated, "There's too much evidence to discount completely the possibility that there's something still in there."[7]

I had yet to find a connection between this treasure and the KGC template, but I was not giving up, and I continued searching for other known treasures. Researching the next location would lead to information that continues to amaze me to this day.

3 BRUTON PARISH CHURCH

AMERICA'S ROSSLYN CHAPEL?

While studying the legends of Victorio Peak, I came across some information regarding potential treasure, said to have been buried on the grounds of the Bruton Parish Church in Williamsburg, Virginia. The church, with its ties to history and our Founding Fathers, can be labeled a treasure in its own right. The city of Williamsburg was said to have played an important role in the American Revolution, and several of our nation's most well-known patriots attended this church. "Among the men of the Revolution who attended Bruton Parish Church were Thomas Jefferson, George Washington, Richard Henry Lee, George Wythe, Patrick Henry, and George Mason."[1]

As I stated before, very few treasure stories seem to be useful for anything other than entertaining campfire tales. At first glance, the story of the Bruton Vault appeared to be the granddaddy of all campfire tales. It involves Francis Bacon, who has been called the father of modern science, Freemasonry, Rosicrucians, and more. Some even link his identity with Shakespeare. This one seemed to have all the makings of a first-class conspiracy theory! I couldn't help myself; I just had to read all about it, and I am glad I did.

Before I start, I would like to explain what a Rosicrucian is to those

Fig. 3.1. Old Bruton Church, Williamsburg, Virginia, ca. 1775

who don't know. One of the best descriptions I have found comes from Peter Dawkins, a recognized authority on the Rosicrucians of the sixteenth and seventeenth centuries, who states: "The Rosicrucians were known as Navigators—the ones who planned the routes, mapped the stars and steered the ships on their journeys of exploration. The journeys, however, were not just worldly journeys on Earth but also metaphysical journeys of the mind. Besides being called Navigators, the Rosicrucians were also known as the invisible Brethren, for they were privy to esoteric knowledge and worked, as it were, in disguise openly or behind the scenes."[2]

In her book *Foundations Unearthed,* Maria Bauer (who later married 33rd-degree Freemason Manly P. Hall, author of *The Secret Teachings of All Ages*) describes how she decoded ciphers in books and on gravestones that led her to the discovery of the original foundations of Bruton Parish Church, which she uncovered in 1938, proving her information was correct. But the information also led to the location of an underground vault 20 feet below the original foundations. Her work was halted, and she was not allowed to continue her excavation of the site. The contents of the vault are said to hold the answers to secrets that would be of great value to both the world in general and to Freemasons. In the foreword to Bauer's book, the respected Masonic scholar Harold V. B. Voorhis wrote, "I have undertaken to introduce Maria Bauer to the Masonic scholars because it appears to me that we are on the brink of finding the answer to 'from whence we came.'"[3]

Voorhis adds, "In the past, codes and cyphers have been found in the Shakespeare works, and from evidence at hand additional ones will be found—but this code is the first which has had a physical proof. This is borne out of discovering, in the code, the existence of the old Bruton Church and then, by excavation, authenticating the code messages. With this example, it is not difficult to conceive that many far-reaching discoveries will result."[4]

So now come the questions regarding the contents of the Bruton Vault and who placed them there. The answers are said to start with Queen Elizabeth I and Robert Dudley, son of John Dudley, Duke of Northumberland. Both Elizabeth and Robert were prisoners in the Tower of London in 1554–55. Elizabeth was imprisoned "under suspicion of treason for planning to secure the throne to the Protestant Succession, and Robert for helping his father attempt to place Lady Jane Grey (who was married to his son, Guilford Dudley) on the throne. Jane and Guilford were beheaded. Elizabeth and [Robert] Dudley fell in love when they met at the Tower and were secretly married in 1557. In *Francis Bacon: Last of the Tudors,* Deventer von Kunow records that the chronicles of the Tower of London reveal that there was a marriage ceremony between the two which had been performed by a visiting monk."[5] They are said to have had a child several years later and that child is said to have been none other than *the* Francis Bacon.

For various political reasons, Francis's parentage was kept secret, and he was raised by his foster parents, Sir Nicholas Bacon and his wife, Lady Anne Bacon, who was well educated and knew the Bible very well. She is said to have had a great influence on Francis. At the age of twelve, Francis attended Trinity College, Cambridge, and it is here that Queen Elizabeth I was said to have secretly acknowledged him as her son and instructed him to never use his real identity. David Allen Rivera, a Bruton Vault skeptic, writes in his book *Mystery at Colonial Williamsburg: The Truth of Bruton Vault* that several years later, when Francis was sixteen years of age, "he was sent to Paris (with English Ambassador Sir Amyas Paulet on the large ship known as the Dreadnought) to study Egyptian, Arabian, Indian and Greek philosophy with particular attention given to the Ancient Mysteries and their Ritual Rites. He learned how ciphers were used secretly in diplomatic affairs, and personally wrote that while he was in Paris, he created a secret cipher system that could be inserted into a document without arousing suspicion. . . . While living in Europe, Francis Bacon was initiated into the mysterious Order of the Knights Templar."[6]

In his book *The Secret Teachings of All Ages,* Manly Palmer Hall writes:

Father of modern science, remodeler of modern law, editor of the modern Bible, patron of modern democracy, and one of the founders of modern Freemasonry, Sir Francis Bacon was a man of many aims and purposes. He was a Rosicrucian; some have intimated *the* Rosicrucian. If not actually the Illustrious Father C.R.C. referred to in the Rosicrucian manifestoes, he was certainly a high initiate of the Rosicrucian Order, and it is his activities in connection with the secret body that are of prime importance to students of symbolism, philosophy, and literature.

Scores of volumes have been written to establish Sir Francis Bacon as the real author of the plays and sonnets popularly ascribed to William Shakespeare. An impartial consideration of these documents cannot but convince the open-minded of the verisimilitude of the Baconian theory. In fact, those enthusiasts who for years have struggled to identify Sir Francis Bacon as the true "Bard of Avon" might long since have won their case had they emphasized its most important angle, namely, that Sir Francis Bacon, the Rosicrucian initiate, wrote into the Shakespearian plays the secret teachings of the Fraternity of R.C. and the true rituals of the Freemasonic Order, of which order it may yet be discovered that he was the actual founder.[7]

With all those accomplishments, Francis Bacon was definitely a driven man. Given his situation, he had the means to accomplish his goals, and at the top of his list were, according to Manly P. Hall, "universal education and universal democracy." Bacon is said to have viewed the New World as an opportunity to turn those goals into a reality. In fact, Bacon wrote a book titled *New Atlantis: A Worke Unfinished,* in which he describes the fictional land of Bensalem, where the inhabitants value education, democracy, generosity, and enlightenment. They thrive on advancements from the sciences conducted through an organization of researchers based in what is called Salomon's [*sic*] House. It is this book, many claim, that laid the template for what the United States was meant to be.

What is in the alleged vault? According to Marie Bauer Hall, the treasure consists of works and documents regarding topics such as religion, philosophy, and the histories of Freemasonry, the Rosicrucians, Europe, and America, as well as other writings and documents of great historical significance.

It is an incredible story, and it almost seems too fantastic to be true—but is it possible? Keeping an open mind, I had to say yes, it is possible. Is it true? I wasn't sure, so I tried looking at it from a different angle.

There are also said to be tunnels connecting to the Bruton Vault. Some of these are said to connect to the Wren Chapel in the Wren Building (constructed between the years of 1695 and 1700) of the College of William and Mary, which is located approximately 1,715 feet west of the alleged location of the hidden vault. That number, 1,715, caught my eye. Bruton Parish Church has been built three times in its history, the most recent of which was in the year 1715. Maybe that's just a coincidence? But it showed up again when I measured the distance from Bruton Parish Church to Victorio Peak. The distance between the two locations is 1,715 miles.

The Wren Building is named in honor of the famous architect Sir Christopher Wren. Born six and a half years after the death of Francis Bacon, Wren was a founding member of the prestigious Royal Society, Britain's distinguished scientific organization. There has been debate throughout the years about whether or not Wren was a Freemason; however, after reading an article by Freemason H. L. Haywood in a copy of the *Builder Magazine* published in 1924, I believe it is highly probable that Sir Christopher Wren was a Freemason. Haywood writes: "Thus, the minutes of a meeting held on June 3, 1723, give the substance of what the brethren had decided: 'The set of mahogany candlesticks presented to this lodge by its worthy old Master, Sir Christopher Wren, ordered to be carefully deposited in a wooden case lin'd [*sic*] with cloth to be immediately purchased for the purpose.'"[8]

There are also claims that Wren was a Rosicrucian, a Christian Kabbalist, and an adherent of the philosophy of Francis Bacon. The Royal Society was often referred to as the Invisible College and as Solomon's House. The Invisible College is also often used as another name for the Rosicrucian order. It is not a physical structure, but rather a sharing of knowledge, theories, and ideas in secret and safe from persecution in a time when going against an accepted ideology could literally cost a person their head. The other name, Solomon's House, differs only slightly in spelling from the name of the academies of scientific research in Bacon's *New Atlantis*. I am of the opinion that Wren and at least some of his peers at the Royal Society were a powerful continuation of the ideology and goals of Francis Bacon.

The web page for Colonial Williamsburg states that "the College of William and Mary's Christopher Wren Building is the oldest academic structure still in use in America."[9] It goes on to say that George Washington was at one time chancellor of the college and that Thomas

Jefferson was a student there. Both were Freemasons. Regarding Wren's connections with the building that bears his name, the site also states that "the Reverend Hugh Jones, a William and Mary mathematics professor, wrote in 1724 that the College Building was 'modeled by Sir Christopher Wren.'"[10]

The logo used by the Bruton Parish Church Foundation bears a striking resemblance to the KGC template. It is the design of the large window located on the church's east side (see fig. 3.2). According to a report by Bullock on the Colonial Williamsburg website, "The facade of the church, facing Palace Green has been returned to its precise appearance of the eighteenth century. Its brickwork was least disturbed by repairs. Its (The East facade) window based on a measured drawing is the same that was installed when the East addition was made in 1752."[11]

The window design was intriguing, but it may be nothing more than just a pretty design. Even if there is a connection, I still needed a scale and more treasure locations in order to attempt to use the template to find my great-great-grandfather's treasure.

It's quite obvious that Freemasonry and Rosicrucianism played an important role in the lives of the men associated with the Bruton Vault story. They lived in a time when stepping out of line, especially in the realm of religion or politics, could quite literally cost you your life. The leaders of the Catholic Church were well known in those days for having people executed or, at the very least, ruining the lives of people who expressed views that contradicted their own. It boiled down to power. If brilliant men like Francis Bacon, Christopher Wren, and many others of their caliber were to have a voice of any kind to express their ideas, research, and findings without fear of death, to pass on knowledge that for millennia had been withheld by corrupt powers bent on controlling the thoughts and ideas of the masses, then they needed to do so in secret, at first. I believe Francis Bacon's *New Atlantis* was written not only as a means of expressing his desire for a free, democratic society and universal education but also as a call to action for like-minded souls. The vehicles in which they chose

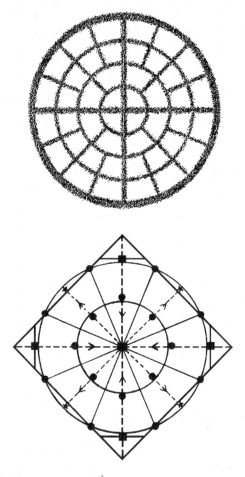

Fig. 3.2. Comparison of window in the eastern end of the
Bruton Parish Church (above) and the KGC template (below)

to accomplish this great work appear to have been Freemasonry and
other associated societies.

Looking at this mystery from another angle provided more information and additional clues. The number 1,715 appeared to tie into this
somehow, and I needed to research that along with the evidence pointing to Wren, his peers, and Francis Bacon. It is apparent that they were
Freemasons and had ties with Rosicrucianism. I believe those societies
play an important role in this story, but my original questions regarding

the KGC template and my family's treasure map remained unanswered. That said, knowing my great-great-grandfather was also a Freemason, I came to the conclusion that if I were going to have a chance at finding the treasure in his map, I would likely need to research all I could regarding Freemasonry, Rosicrucians, and other like-minded societies.

4 CONNECTING THE DOTS

Shortly after my mother wrote *Jesse James Lived and Died in Texas,* we were contacted by many people armed with stories of Jesse James, treasure, and sometimes both. Most of the treasure stories turned out to be tall tales, but there are a few that turned out to be true.

One of those true stories came from a man by the name of George Roming from El Paso, Texas. We got to know George well, and after a few years he wanted to tell us his amazing story. George Roming, a 32nd-degree Freemason, Shriner, and World War II veteran, was born in 1920, not far from where Jesse James aka James Lafayette Courtney lived in the small rural community of Buttermilk, Texas, later renamed Blevins. As a young boy and later a teenager, George would walk past Jesse's farm. When Jesse saw him, he would invite him to sit on the front porch and talk for a while. They got to know one another, and Jesse trusted him. In the 1930s, Jesse had George swear an oath of secrecy and hired him to help move 700 bars of gold. George said that after they had transported the gold in a large wagon to a ranch owned by one of Jesse's friends, Jesse removed 20 bars for himself. This friend's ranch was approximately 20 miles away. When they arrived, they were met by two other old men and two boys around George's age. They buried the gold in a rectangular field. They found the center of the field, and from that center, Jesse paced 40 steps to the north and instructed

27

them to dig a hole approximately 8 feet in depth. They lined the bottom of the hole with large timbers, unloaded the gold into the hole, covered it up, and left.

When asked if the other two boys could have ever told anyone, George replied that he knew for a fact that they had not. He did not elaborate, adding that he was only telling us because he was the only one left, he trusted us, and we were Jesse's descendants. George drew a map for us on a piece of brown paper and described to us exactly where they buried the gold. The place he described is now under Lake Belton, which was created in 1954 by the United States Army Corps of Engineers. When I informed George of this, he gritted his teeth, looked down, and shook his head in disappointment. George Roming died in 2007 at the age of eighty-six. He was a good man and a good friend.

A little more than a year after we met George, we were contacted by Nita Callahan. She was associated with former Texas State Attorney General Waggoner Carr, and she wanted to show us the locations of two treasures that had been recovered. We were not disappointed. The first site was located in Georgetown, Texas, approximately 2.5 miles west of the Williamson County courthouse. It was said to have held a very large cache of gold bars weighing close to 80 pounds each. I found it strange that the gold was said to have been Spanish gold, even though it was allegedly a KGC treasure cache.

Hearing "Spanish gold," I immediately thought of Victorio Peak in New Mexico. When I returned home I pulled out the maps and started drawing lines. As I stated before, the line from Victorio Peak to the Bruton Parish Church is 1,715 miles long. I then drew a line from Victorio Peak to the site near Georgetown, Texas. That line is 548 miles long, and the angle off the main line (the line from Victorio Peak to the Bruton Parish Church) is 33 degrees. I don't know about you, but to me there seemed to be a lot of coincidences here. Not only is the number 33 associated with Freemasonry, but it also happens to be the number of Bacon (as in Francis Bacon) when using gematria along with the Elizabethan alphabet of his day.* But the lines had no resemblance to the lines on the so-called KGC template.

The second site Mrs. Callahan showed us was located to the northeast, on a property next to a cemetery almost 1 mile south-southwest of the main intersection in Little River-Academy, Texas. While the treasure that used to be located on this site was smaller than the one in Georgetown, it was said to have been worth millions of dollars in gold alone. We were told that a railroad track was laid there and was used to unload the treasure into an underground vault. The remains of the track were clearly visible, and the earth around the location of the recovered treasure was marked by a large depression. Although the treasures had long since been recovered, knowing the locations provided valuable information that could possibly help in locating the treasure indicated in my great-great-grandfather's map.

Each time I learned of a treasure site, I would plot the location on a map and work with the KGC template to see if it fit or not. It was not until just over a year later, when I learned of yet another treasure site, that it all started to fall into place. This alleged treasure site is located on the outskirts of the small town of Tow, Texas. Tow (pronounced Tau) is on the eastern side of Llano County, Texas, near where the Colorado River runs into Lake Buchanan. One of the stories connected with this treasure is that a mule train carrying a government payroll was ambushed, and the gold was brought to this location and deposited. It is said to be booby trapped with water, the water being provided by the nearby Colorado River.

Now, in addition to the Victorio Peak and Bruton Vault sites, I had four treasure sites in Texas to work with, but I couldn't figure out how or if they would fit the template. Searching for more answers to the questions that were piling up, I had to ask myself, who buried

---

*Gematria is a method of placing a numerical value on Hebrew letters and words. The Elizabethan alphabet consisted of 24 letters. Simply put, the letters *i* and *j* were the same, as were the letters *u* and *v*. Our modern English alphabet contains 26 letters.

these treasures? George Roming told me that he had helped my great-great-grandfather bury one. The others are said to have been Spanish and/or KGC treasures. I personally don't believe that the gold found in Georgetown, Texas, or Victorio Peak in New Mexico was Spanish treasure, nor do I believe it was a KGC treasure cache. Some of it may have been put in place by Spaniards, but I seriously doubt the Spanish Crown or any other government had any knowledge of it. But at the time I tried to find a logical explanation of how the alleged treasure vault at the Bruton Parish Church in Williamsburg, said to have been laid there by the successors of the Englishman Francis Bacon, could have had anything to do with Spanish or KGC treasure in New Mexico and Texas. I also wondered if the Georgetown site had any connections with the Bruton Vault and the Victorio Peak treasures. The numbers 33 and 1,715 associated with the sites might just be a strange coincidence, but I felt it warranted more research just to make sure. If the sites are connected, then what is the connection shared by Jesse James aka James Lafayette Courtney, Albert Pike, Francis Bacon, and the Spaniards? If they are connected, then there must be a common link. The only answer I had—and it felt as if I was going way out on a limb—was Freemasonry.

If Freemasons were responsible for burying these treasures, then the next obvious question would have to be why? What purpose could they or anyone else have had for burying so much wealth? Looking back through history, we can find many examples of why someone or some group with so much wealth would feel the need to bury it for safekeeping. One such example would be the Knights Templar.

5 SIGNATURES IN NUMBERS

I searched and prayed for answers, and eventually some pieces of the puzzle started to fall into place. I was beginning to uncover the scale of the so-called KGC template. My next step was to prove or disprove the truth about what I had worked so long and hard to discover. I marked several of the closest properties where the template, when laid over a map, indicates locations that treasure caches should be located. I contacted the landowners, informed them of my belief that there may be buried treasure on their property, and asked for permission to search. People react differently to such requests, and I was met with reactions ranging from disbelief to greed and suspicion. I can't say I blame them, as the evening news is full of stories of scams and buried treasure that sound like something that is too good to be true. I've had some people grant me permission, only to change their minds overnight, giving vague, rushed reasons. Later I would learn that they were looking for it on their own. The properties I asked to search were large properties— well over 100 acres—and I never gave away a location. If I did, they wouldn't have any need for me, and I would be left without either a treasure or the satisfaction of knowing whether or not I was right. After having several encounters like that, I decided to take some time to search for more answers.

As I mentioned in the previous chapter, the only answer I had in regard to who was responsible for burying the treasures was the Freemasons. In order to prove or disprove this theory, I had a lot of research to do. What started off as an attempt to locate my great-great-grandfather's treasure had transformed not only into a treasure hunt but also into a quest for knowledge, and the thirst for knowledge seemed more powerful for me than the possibility of striking it rich. Sure, I would love to have some gold or silver, but searching for answers to a mystery like this gave me a feeling of being connected to something much greater than wealth. It left me feeling as if I shared a connection of sorts with people who lived centuries before me.

In researching Freemasonry, I started with Albert Pike. Pike was a 33rd-degree Freemason, a captain in the United States Cavalry, a brigadier general in the Confederate Army, author, attorney, teacher, scholar, and explorer. It is rumored that he was a member of the Knights of the Golden Circle, but I have yet to see any proof of that. A quick online search reveals that Albert Pike is a favorite among conspiracy theorists, who make a habit of taking his quotes out of context, misquoting him altogether, and citing his mention of Kabbalah and the double-headed eagle on the cover of his book as if they are positive proof that he was an evil and sinister man. That said, I am glad they pointed me toward the Kabbalah and other topics, which would later provide me with some of the answers I had been searching for. Prior to that, my only concept of Kabbalah was that it was something practiced by the Hollywood crowd and involved the use of a red string tied around celebrity wrists.

In reading Pike's book, *Morals and Dogma of the Ancient and Accepted Scottish Rite of Freemasonry,* I noticed that while Pike covers many philosophical lines of thought as they pertain to the 32 degrees of Scottish Rite Freemasonry, he mentions Kabbalah throughout the text. Here I will offer three of the many quotes regarding Kabbalah that made an impression on me:

Pythagoras, the great divulger of the philosophy of numbers, visited all the sanctuaries of the world. He went into Judaea, where he procured himself to be circumcised, that he might be admitted to the secrets of the Kabalah, which the prophets Ezekiel and Daniel, not without some reservations, communicated to him. Then, not without some difficulty, he succeeded in being admitted to the Egyptian initiation, upon the recommendation of King Amasis. The power of his genius supplied the deficiencies of the imperfect communications of the Hierophants, and he himself became a Master and a revealer.[1]

The Kabalistic doctrine was long the religion of the Sage and the Savant; because, like Freemasonry, it incessantly tends toward spiritual perfection, and the fusion of the creeds and Nationalities of Mankind. In the eyes of the Kabalist, all men are his brothers; and their relative ignorance is, to him, but a reason for instructing them. There were illustrious Kabalists among the Egyptians and Greeks, whose doctrines the Orthodox Church has accepted; and among the Arabs were many, whose wisdom was not slighted by the Mediaeval Church.[2]

How completely the Temple of Solomon was symbolic, is manifest, not only from the continual reproduction in it of the sacred numbers and of astrological symbols in the historical descriptions of it; but also, and yet more, from the details of the imaginary reconstructed edifice, seen by Ezekiel in his vision. The Apocalypse completes the demonstration, and shows the kabalistic meanings of the whole. The Symbola Architectonica are found on the most ancient edifices; and these mathematical figures and instruments, adopted by the Templars, and identical with those on the gnostic seals and abraxæ, connect their dogma with the Chaldaic, Syriac, and Egyptian Oriental philosophy. The secret Pythagorean doctrines of numbers were preserved by the monks of Thibet, by the Hierophants of Egypt and Eleusis, at Jerusalem, and in the circular Chapters of the Druids; and they are especially consecrated in that mysterious book, the Apocalypse of Saint John.[3]

The three quotes above describe Kabbalah or gematria as a philosophy of numbers. If we applied the concept to the English alphabet, placing numerical values on each letter, starting with the letter *A* as 1 and *Z* as 26, the number 1, spelled *one*, would have a numerical value of 34. Gematria is more complex than that, but hopefully, that gives you the basic idea if you are unfamiliar with the concept. Here's a description of gematria from Rabbi Yitzchak Ginsburgh:

In Hebrew, each letter possesses a numerical value. Gematria is the calculation of the numerical equivalence of letters, words, or phrases, and, on that basis, gaining, insight into interrelation of different concepts and exploring the interrelationship between words and ideas.

The assumption behind this technique is that numerical equivalence is not coincidental. Since the world was created through God's "speech," each letter represents a different creative force. Thus, the numerical equivalence of two words reveals an internal connection between the creative potentials of each one.[4]

Pike's mention of the similarities between Kabbalah and Freemasonry, seeking spiritual perfection as well as the fusion of the nationalities and creeds of man, sounds very similar to the ideas suggested by Francis Bacon in his *New Atlantis*. Pike goes on to mention the Temple of Solomon, the Knights Templar, astrological symbols, and sacred numbers. He suggests that the Bible contains secret Pythagorean—that is, Kabbalistic—doctrines of numbers, along with the vision of Ezekiel in which the prophet has a vision of the rebuilt Temple in Jerusalem. Often referred to as the New Jerusalem, it also resonates with Bacon's *New Atlantis*.

Kabbalah comes from a Hebrew verb meaning *to receive* and it has been referred to as *the soul of the Torah.* Two other forms of Kabbalah have emanated from the original Jewish version. The first is the Christian Kabbalah and the second is a mix of Western mysticism derived from Jewish, Egyptian, and Christian sources. (Sometimes the spellings *Kabbalah, Cabala,* and *Qabalah* are used to refer to these three versions, respectively.) In looking for answers to my questions, I've drawn from all three.

After reading through Pike's book *Morals and Dogma,* I had no doubt that the double-headed eagle on the cover was more than just a pretty symbol. As Pike stated, "The ancient symbols and allegories always had more than one interpretation. They always had a double

Fig. 5.1. Logo on Albert Pike's *Morals and Dogma*

meaning, and sometimes more than two, one serving as the envelope of the other."[5] I found the answer to at least one of the meanings in a book titled *Masonic Writings* by Freemason Gregory H. Peters. In his conclusion he states: "The double-headed eagle, as the ensign of the Alchemical Rebus or Stone of the Philosophers, symbolizes this process, the magnum opus or Great Work of spiritual regeneration. Through its unification of opposites and association with alchemical Fire, the path of regeneration and ascent up the Tree of Life is indicated."[6]

The Tree of Life is one of the most fundamental symbols of Kabbalah. It consists of twenty-two paths, corresponding with the twenty-two letters of the Hebrew alphabet. The paths move through ten sefiroth and one hidden sefiroth (there are varied spellings) or spheres that serve as channels of Divine energy and are arranged in a specific order. "According to Dion Fortune, the Tree of Life is the most comprehensive meditative symbol of the Western Esoteric Tradition, and is an archive of science, psychology, philosophy and theology. Compare to de Lubicz's description of the Egyptian Temple as a 'library in stone.' Fulcanelli and others use the same language to describe the Gothic Cathedrals in Europe."[7]

At this point, though I knew the scale of the KGC template, I was not sure how or even if the scale of the KGC template connected with the Bruton Vault and Victorio Peak sites. As stated before, the distance from the Bruton Parish Church to Victorio Peak is 1,715 miles, and that number showed up in other ways around Williamsburg. After studying more about Kabbalah and reading of the philosophy of numbers in Pike's *Morals and Dogma*, I decided that if the two sites were connected, then the numbers (distances and dates) could have significant meaning.

I started with the two numbers I had to work with in relation to the Bruton Vault, Victorio Peak, and the site near Georgetown, Texas: 1,715, the distance between the Bruton Parish Church and Victorio Peak; and 548, the distance between Victorio Peak and the Georgetown site. The prime factors of 1,715 are $5 \times 7 \times 7 \times 7$. In terms of Kabbalah, the number 5 is connected with the Hebrew letter heh (ה), whose meanings include *to be broken; to take seed; behold or revelation.*[8]* Heh is also used twice in the ineffable name of the Creator: יהוה or YHWH. Because the name is so sacred, many Kabbalists use the heh to represent the name of God.

The number 7 is connected with the letter zayin (ז), whose meanings include *weapon; sword; ornament* or *crown; species; gender; to sustain.*[9] Another way of representing 1,715 is 5 × 343, where 343 is the gematria value of the Hebrew geshem, which in Hebrew can mean *rain, to realize,* and *sustenance.* While this was helpful, I wasn't able to perceive any connections with what I was searching for until I found a book titled *777 and other Qabalistic Writings of Aleister Crowley.* The cover and title had me wondering what 777 had to do with the Tree of Life. I was pleasantly surprised. The 22 paths in the Tree of Life are numbered 11 through 32. The gematria or numerical value of the numbers of the paths totals 777. This was important, as 777 could be construed as representing the path one travels through the Tree of Life from our physical state to the spiritual, or from Earth to Heaven. It shows the way from God to creation or from man to God. The distance from Bruton Parish Church to Victorio Peak, 1,715 miles, can then be represented as 5 × 343 or 5 × 7 × 7 × 7, which can be understood as meaning *God and the Tree of Life* or *Behold, the Tree of Life.* This was an important clue supporting my theory of the Tree of Life template. The 22 paths follow a certain order through the Tree of Life, which is often called the Path of the Flaming Sword, likely referring to this verse in the Old Testament: "So he drove out the man; and he placed at the east of the garden of Eden Cherubims, and a flaming sword which turned every way, to keep the way of the tree of life" (Genesis 3:24; this and other biblical quotations are taken from the King James Version). Another

---

*The transliterations of the names of the Hebrew letters vary widely in their spelling: *heh* can also be rendered as *hei* or *he,* for example, while the letter *yod* (Y) can be transliterated as *yud.*

way of interpreting this path is to view it as a buffer between God and all of creation. In a Kabbalistic view, the Divine energy used in creation flows down through this path, and in our attempts to become closer to God, we are to travel the same path from the bottom up.

With all of that, I thought I had my answer. The number 1,715 can be translated as *Behold, the Tree of Life*. It can be symbolic of a blessing. It can also mean *to take seed,* as if the Tree of Life were taking seed and sprouting roots. This in turn can be viewed as a metaphor for burying the treasures in a template formed by the shape of the Tree of Life.

The second number I had to work with was 548, the distance between Victorio Peak and the Georgetown site. The number 548 can be expressed as 4×137. The number 4 is signified by the letter daleth in Hebrew, and it too has several meanings. It can mean *door, poor man,* or *lifting up.* As for the number 137, that happens to be the gematria for the word *Kabbalah.*

The number 7 carries some additional significance in this because of its various meanings, including *sword* and *crown. Sword* can refer to the Path of the Flaming Sword in the Tree of Life, and Kether, the name of the first *sefirah** or sphere at the top of the Tree of Life, means *crown.* Another meaning for the number 5 is *broken,* which would indicate the column in the center of the Tree of Life, which was broken when man fell from grace. Man, having lost his ability to speak directly to God, now must travel through the correct channels in his attempt to reunite with the Divine (see fig. 5.2).

The central pillar in the Tree of Life, from Crown to Kingdom, represents the line from Bruton Parish Church to Victorio Peak and is 1,715 miles in length. The path from Malkuth (Kingdom) to Netzach

---

*Sefirah (plural *sefiroth*) is a Hebrew word for which there is no exact equivalent in English. It probably comes from the root *sefer,* meaning *to count* or *number,* although some have linked it to the Greek *sphaira* or *sphere.* It refers to the ten emanations of God on the Kabbalistic Tree of Life, plus the one "nonsefirah," Da'ath or Knowledge (which will be discussed later).

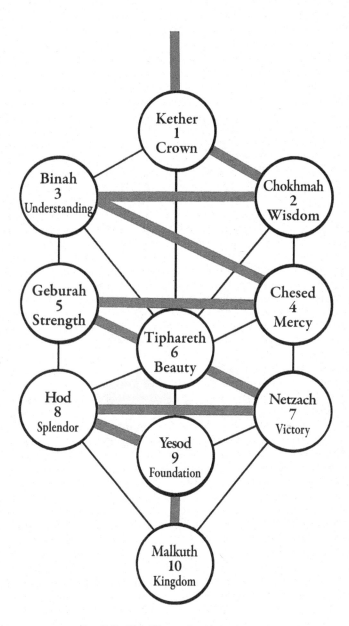

Fig. 5.2. The Tree of Life showing
the ten sefiroth and the
Path of the Flaming Sword (thicker line).

(Victory), or Georgetown, Texas, to Victorio Peak, is 548 miles in length.

What about the other numbers? The outer pillars, from Wisdom to Victory and from Understanding to Splendor, are each 924 miles long. The number 924 can be represented as 4 × 231. I've mentioned the number 4 or daleth being defined as a door, so what about the number 231? The number 231 is associated with the *Sefer Yetzirah*, translated in English as *The Book of Formation*, the first and oldest text relating to Kabbalah. "The 231 gates of *Sefer Yetzirah* refer to the 231 two-letter combinations of the 22 letters of the Hebrew alphabet. (This refers to combinations of different letters only.)"[10] The 231 gates of the Sefer Yetzirah are said to be used when God uses the Tree of Life in the act of creation of something, anything spiritual or physical. "As the Creator enters and enlivens the Hebrew Tree, the 231 Gates of Formation are generated, descending into and filling Yetzirah."[11] This could be viewed as those who buried the treasures, invoking the aid of God in helping them in their plan to create this *New Atlantis* and bring it into reality.

Another aspect of the Tree of Life is the three pillars and the attributes that have been assigned to them. The right side (Wisdom, Mercy, and Victory) is the masculine side. The left side (Understanding, Strength, and Splendor) is the feminine side, and the center pillar (Crown, Beauty, Foundation, and Kingdom) is considered to be the point of equilibrium between the masculine and feminine pillars. I found it very interesting that on a modern map (see fig. 5.3), the top of the right pillar (the masculine side) is very near the city of Columbus, Georgia (a masculine name). The top of the left pillar (the feminine side) is very close to Columbia City, Indiana (a feminine name). The top of the center pillar is where the sefirah Crown is located. This is in Williamsburg, Virginia, the location of the second-oldest college in America—the College of William and Mary, named for King William III and Queen Mary II of England, both of whom signed the charter to form the college. King, queen, male and female; it fits the

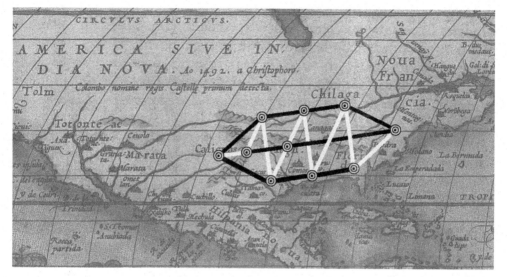

Fig. 5.3. Diagram of the Tree of Life overlaid on the
North American portion of a world map from 1570

requirements for equilibrium in the center pillar as well as the sefirah
designated Crown.

It isn't much of a stretch to think that Francis Bacon, a master of cryptography, student of philosophies and religions, father of
modern science, and alleged founder of modern Freemasonry and
Rosicrucianism, along with his peers and successors, who were some
of the brightest minds in European history, could have devised such
a plan. The numbers shown appear to be a signature, not of one man
but of a group or groups of people, holding a similar mind-set and putting their ideas into action. The time was right: they planted the seeds
of Bacon's New Atlantis so that it could become a reality, transfer-
ring wealth and knowledge to the New World to be buried there and
marking the locations on a template of the Tree of Life. When the time
was right and the information and wealth could be used responsibly, it
could be uncovered and put into use.

Imagine standing at the Bruton Parish Church, facing west
and able to view the lines of the template forming the Tree of Life.
Knowing the information regarding the numbers 1,715 and 548, we

can almost hear the numbers scream out, "Behold, the Tree of Life," beckoning us to enter the door leading down the Kabbalistic Path of the Flaming Sword.

But what about the KGC template? How does it fit in with this Tree of Life template? I believe it has everything to do with the Tree of Life and very little to do with the KGC.

6 THE THREE VEILS

Throughout the years, I've heard many treasure stories from the United States and other countries. While Texas has more than its fair share, size for size, legends in Oklahoma seem to rival those of Texas—and like Texas, Oklahoma has a lot of tall tales. After separating the wheat from the chaff and relying on evidence from reliable sources, I wondered if the template worked in other areas too. If it did, would the scale remain the same, or did it change with different areas? Did each treasure location have the same template, and if so, did the templates for those areas share the same scale?

After determining whether or not a story was reliable, I applied the same method that worked for me with the template in central Texas and marked any alleged buried treasure locations on a map. Then I would lay a transparency of the template over the map to see if it worked or not. Several times it seemed to work, and it was the same scale. Zooming out and viewing a map of the United States, I noticed that not only was the scale the same, but it lined up with the template I had marked in central Texas. I wanted to see if the templates in Texas connected with the templates in Oklahoma. I was amazed when I found that yes, they did connect.

When someone is laying out a city or a design, the logical thing to do is to lay out a grid, not just to keep things orderly but also to make it easier to find what you're looking for. Applying that logic to multiple buried treasures seems to make perfect sense. Anyone burying a treasure would want to make sure that not only they but their peers or successors can find it. Land and its topography change over the years due to erosion, floods, fires, and other forces. While a simple map may work for a few short years, over a period of a decade or more, the land can change in appearance, making the map virtually useless. For this reason, laying out a grid design makes perfect sense.

When searching for answers, especially when they deal with esoteric topics, it can be very tempting to see connections among noncorresponding aspects of a template or design. Keeping that in mind, my next step involved the numbers that make up the scale and dimensions of the templates. Determining whether or not the numbers in the scale

Fig. 6.1. The template shown in its grid formation

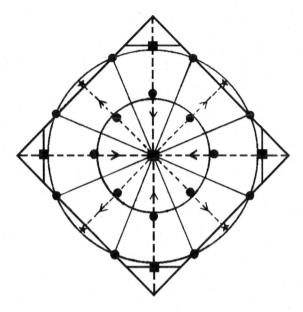

Fig. 6.2. Alleged KGC treasure template

held any Kabbalistic meaning would help me decide whether or not the alleged KGC template was related to the Tree of Life template. I also had questions regarding the shape of this template.

If you count each mark in the template pictured in figure 6.2 (squares, dots, stars, and turkey tracks), you will see that there are 33 locations. Thirty-three, like the angle on the line from Victorio Peak to Georgetown off the center line that travels from Victorio Peak to the Bruton Parish Church. As stated earlier, the number for *Bacon,* as in Francis Bacon, is 33. Furthermore, there are 33 degrees in Scottish Rite Freemasonry, and the cover of Albert Pike's book is adorned with a double-headed eagle with the number 33 above it. As we learned earlier, author Gregory H. Peters writes that the double-headed eagle can be associated with the Tree of Life. The number 33 is held as a mystical number of importance among several religious beliefs and societies. For example, the first Temple of Solomon stood unmolested for 33 years before it was pillaged, King David ruled for 33 years, and Christ was crucified at the age of 33. And then there's the Tree of Life with its

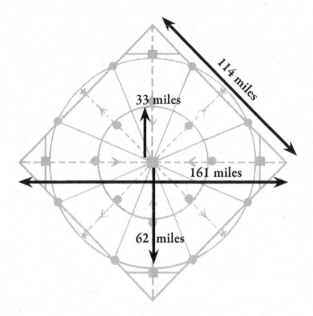

Fig. 6.3. Large Veil template

10 sefiroth and 22 paths, which totals 32, but if we add the hidden sefirah Da'ath or Knowledge (which we will discuss later), we have a total of 33. According to Rabbi Yitzchak Ginsburg of the Gal Enai website, the number 33 is also the value of the Hebrew word for *open* or *reveal*.

Traveling around the square in figure 6.3, each corner is 114 miles apart. From the center of the template to the inner circle is 33 miles, and it is 62 miles to the outer circle. The diagonal of the square, which runs from corner to corner through the interior of the square, is 161 miles, the number we will examine first.

The Great Year or the Platonic Year (named after the ancient Greek philosopher Plato, who first discussed it) is based on the precession of the equinoxes, the time that it takes for the constellations to appear to rotate around the Earth. One complete precession takes approximately 25,920 years, the square root of which is 160.99 or 161. If we multiply 161 × 2, we get the number 322, and looking at Genesis 3:22 in the Bible, we find another connection with the Tree of Life: "And the Lord God said, Behold, the man is become as one of us, to know good and evil: and now, lest he put forth his hand, and take also of the tree of life, and eat, and live for ever." The number 322 is also the gematria for *the original man* (when spelled in English), often called the primordial man or Adam Kadmon, whose body is said to be represented by the Tree of Life.

I found another interesting piece of information regarding the number 161 in an article by the sixteenth-century Kabbalist Yitzchak Luria. The article says that "the name *Eh-yeh* [I am that I am] known by its numerical value 161, or '*Kasa*,' is spelled out as follows: alef (1) lamed (30) pei (80), hei (5) yud (10), yud (10) vav (6) dalet (4), hei (5) yud (10)."[1] The word *Kasa* can be translated as meaning *to cover* or *conceal from view,* as a veil would do.

The inner circle of the template has a radius of 33 miles, thus a diameter of 66 miles. Like the number 161, the number 66 shares a connection with the precession of the equinoxes in that the precession moves at a rate of 1 degree every 66 years, or approximately 10 degrees every 666 years. The magic square of the sun, as described by the sixteenth-century magus Henry Cornelius Agrippa, is made up of 6 cells in width by 6 cells in height. This magic square is numbered 1 through 36, and when all the numbers are added up, they total 666. Another link with the number 66 and the sun is through solar cycles. A solar cycle lasts approximately 11 years, taking 5.5 years, or 66 months, to move from a solar minimum to a solar maximum. There are also 66 books in the Protestant Bible. As stated in 1 Kings 10:14, King Solomon received 666 talents of gold each year.

The outer circle has a radius of 62 miles and a diameter of 124 miles. It corresponds with a cycle involving Venus. Every 124 years, Venus passes between the Earth and the sun and repeats this movement approximately eight years later. Another word sharing the same gematria is the Hebrew word for *Eden* (עדן). Is there any connection between Venus and the Garden of Eden? In Roman mythology, the red rose was created when Jupiter caught Venus bathing. Venus blushed and the white roses near the water turned red from her reflection in the water. In Kabbalah, a rose is said by some to be a symbol for Eden. A rose

Fig. 6.4. Sandro Botticelli's *The Birth of Venus*, ca. 1486

motif can be seen in the beautiful work of Renaissance artist Sandro Botticelli, who painted *The Birth of Venus* in about 1486 (fig. 6.4).

Among the many interpretations of Botticelli's work is one presented by author Charles R. Mack:

> [The] nudity of Venus suggests that of Eve before the Fall as well as the pure love of Paradise. Once landed, the goddess of love will don the earthly garb of mortal sin, an act that will lead to the New Eve—the Madonna whose purity is represented by the nude Venus. Once draped in earthly garments [see the Hora of Spring holding a cloak in the painting] she becomes a personification of the Christian Church which offers a spiritual transport back to the pure love of eternal salvation. In this case the scallop shell upon which this image of Venus/Eve/Madonna/Church stands may be seen in its traditionally symbolic pilgrimage context. Furthermore, the broad expanse of sea serves as a reminder of the Virgin Mary's title *stella maris,* alluding both to the Madonna's name (Maria/Maris)

and to the heavenly body (Venus/Stella). The sea brings forth Venus just as the Virgin gives birth to the ultimate symbol of love, Christ.[2]

Venus is the planetary counterpart to the seventh sefirah, Netzach, and according to Manly P. Hall's *Secret Teachings of All Ages*, the alternative counterpart to the seventh sefirah is is the sun.

Keeping the numbers above in mind, add the symbolism of a circle and square joined together, as representative of the Heavens and Earth joined. Earth is represented by the square and the Heavens by the circle. The Earth and square can also be viewed as male, while the circle and the Heavens can be viewed as female. In fact, many genealogy charts today use the circle and square to represent female and male entries, respectively. The circle and square, or the squaring of the circle, can be viewed as the joining or unity of male and female. The numbers relating to the scale of the inner circle of the template represent the sun, and the numbers of the outer circle represent Venus—again, male and female. God, or equilibrium, is located in the center. Similarly, the pillars of the diagram representing the Tree of Life are represented as feminine and masculine, with equilibrium or harmony in the center.

Another symbol used to represent unity in the joining of male and female, wisdom and knowledge, geometry and God, could be the compass and square of Freemasonry (fig. 6.5). The compass is used to form a circle and the square is self-explanatory. In addition to that, the symbol of the compass and square can be viewed as two triangles, which can be associated with male and female. In the center is the letter G, which is said to represent God, geometry, and/or gnosis (knowledge).

Fig. 6.5. Masonic compass and square

The template also has eight turkey-track symbols that look like this Ⴟ. Four are located within the inner circle, and four are between the inner and outer circles. They look like bird tracks, and I have wondered if they are runic symbols because they match symbols from various ancient runes. Whatever they represent, each of the eight symbols has four points, and 4 × 8 = 32, which falls in line with the 32 paths associated with the Tree of Life (10 sefiroth plus 22 paths) as well as the 32 degrees of Freemasonry, but this will require more research.

We now have the dimensions and explanations of the template, but there are two more templates involved, each one smaller than the previous, meaning there are large, medium, and small templates (fig. 6.6). I have overlaid them on the map, and they too correspond with known treasure and historical sites. The dimensions may represent the three octagons of the Dome of the Rock (see page 107), or the vestibule (large), the sanctuary (medium), and the Holy of Holies (small) of the Temple in Jerusalem.

Fig. 6.6. Large template, showing medium template placements.
Each medium template also contains 9 small templates.

From the center of the medium template to each of the four corners is 24.5 miles, making the diagonal of the square 49 miles across (fig. 6.7). The radius of the inner circle is 10 miles, which means that the inner circle is 20 miles in diameter. The radius of the outer circle is 19 miles, making it 38 miles in diameter. The four sides of the square are each 34.5 miles, giving the square a perimeter of 138 miles.

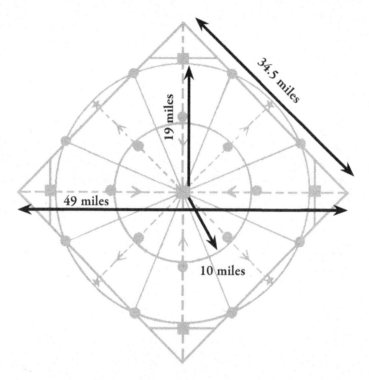

Fig. 6.7. Medium template dimensions

As stated above, the radius of the inner circle of the medium template is 10 miles, making it 20 miles in diameter. Every 20 years Jupiter and Saturn appear to be at the same longitude in the night sky, which is called a *conjunction*. Both planets are masculine symbols.

The radius of the outer circle is 19 miles, corresponding with the 19-year Metonic cycle of our moon. The Greek astronomer Meton of Athens observed that a period of 19 years is almost exactly equal to

235 lunar months and, rounded to full days, counts 6,940 days. Hence this is called the *Metonic cycle*.

The diameter of the outer circle is 38 miles, and the moon also has a 38-year cycle regarding its position. The number 38 is connected to the moon's dual Metonic cycle, used to categorize Celtic stone circles made by Druids. In some examples, 40 stones compose 2 concentric circles, each of 20 stones. Two stones serve as entry markers, leaving 38 remaining.[3]

The number 19 is also the gematria equivalent of Eve (from the Garden of Eden). This further corresponds with the outer circle in the large template, representating Venus and her alleged ties with Eve, as explained in the interpretation of Botticelli's *The Birth of Venus*.

As for the perimeter of this template, I've found references to the number 138: 1 + 3 + 8 = 12, which represents the astrological signs or zodiac and ties back into the number 161, which is the square root of 25,920, the number of years it takes for the 12 constellations of the zodiac to appear to rotate around Earth, also called the precession of the equinoxes. The number 12 also represents the 12 tribes of Israel. The number 12 can be simplified as 1 + 2 = 3, the Holy Trinity of Father, Son, and Holy Spirit; Kether, Chockmah, and Binah in the Tree of Life; or Jesus, Mary Magdalene, and their child (according to certain Gnostic traditions); or other trinities such as Osiris, Isis, and Horus.

The four corners of the small template are 5.5 miles from the center, making the diagonal of the square 11 miles across (fig. 6.8). The radius of the inner circle is 2.25 miles or 4.5 miles in diameter, and the radius of the outer circle is 4.5 miles, giving it a diameter of 9 miles. The perimeter of the square is approximately 34 miles, or 8.5 miles for each of the four sides. The small template fits on the medium template just as the medium fits on the large one, with just one difference: the small template is rotated 7 degrees clockwise.

With 8.5 miles being the length of each, the four sides can be represented as the number 13 (8 + 5 = 13), and 13 × 4 = 52. There are 52 weeks in a year, which links the template to the solar calendar and

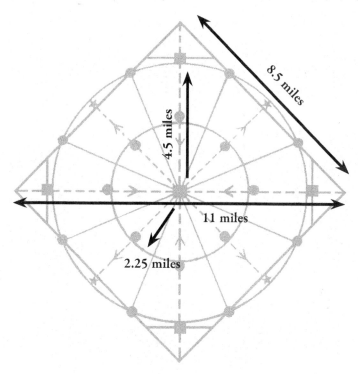

Fig. 6.8. Small template dimensions

the sun. The number 13 is very rich in symbolism throughout various cultures. There were 12 disciples around one Christ for a total of 13. There were 12 tribes of Israel around one God. There are 12 zodiac signs around one sun (see fig. 6.9, page 54). In Kabbalistic thought, there are said to be 13 attributes of Divine mercy. Mary Magdalene is tied to the number 13 not only because her name is made up of 13 letters but also because the letter M is the 13th letter of the Hebrew alphabet as well as the modern English alphabet. Some say that she was the 13th disciple.

Many versions of the Kabbalistic Tree also include astronomical correspondences associated with the various paths and sefiroth. The diameter of the outer circle on the small template, being 9 miles, is one of the more telling aspects of this template. The ninth sefirah on the Tree of Life is labeled Yesod or Foundation and is associated with the moon. Albert Pike has stated that symbols oftentimes carry more than one

Fig. 6.9. Zodiac, from *The Beginnings of Freemasonry*
by Frank C. Higgins

meaning, which certainly applies here. In addition, the small template is 11 miles diagonally from corner to corner, and the number 11 is labeled a "master number" by numerologists. The number 11 can also be symbolic of two pillars, like the pillars named Boaz and Jachin that stood in the porch of Solomon's Temple (1 Kings 7:21), or it could represent the eleventh and hidden sefirah titled Da'ath, Knowledge, or the Abyss, on the Tree of Life. Because it deals with the outer boundaries of this template, 11 could also represent the outer pillars of the Tree of Life.

The dimensions and scale of the templates are rich with symbolism. After years researching this, I have found that they fit not only with various alleged treasure sites but also with historical sites throughout the Americas. While the grid does indeed cover the nation, not every point in the grid has a treasure or historic site. In fact, there are very large areas of the nation that have no treasures associated with the template that I know of; furthermore, it would seem impossible to have that much treasure buried. I believe there may be a system or key to determining what areas have treasure, but I haven't discovered that as of this time.

I had to wonder if the grid itself carried any sort of symbolism. I found my first clue along with a wealth of information presented with an open mind and sober logic regarding many topics including the Tree of Life, Kabbalah, geometry, and more at a website titled "From Pentagram to Pyramids: Masonic and Kabbalistic Symbols in the Washington, DC Map," which was maintained by a man who referred to himself as Big Bytes (though as of this writing, the website account has been suspended).

On this site, the author referred to the story of a man named Offerus: "Before he was a Christian Saint, Christopher was called Offerus, whose only desire was to serve the greatest king on earth. Without going into the whole story, I will point out that at one point Offerus asks a hermit where he could see Christ, and he is told 'everywhere.' At any rate, the image of Offerus, a giant who was 'dull in spirit' carrying Christ over the river is a symbol of the gross matter that carries the gold, while the river is Chaos, the opposite of Form. Note the diamond pattern on Offerus' belt."[4] He directs the reader to *Le mystère des cathédrales* (The mystery of the cathedrals) by the twentieth-century alchemist Fulcanelli:

Offerus' belt is marked with crisscross lines, like those seen on the surface of the solvent when it has been prepared according to canon law. This is the sign, recognized by all the Philosophers as marking exteriorly the intrinsic virtue, the perfection and extreme purity of their mercurial substance. I have already said several times, and I will repeat again, that the whole work of the art consists in processing this mercury until it receives the above-mentioned sign. And this sign has been called by the ancient authors the *Seal of Hermes, Seal of the Wise (Sel des Sages,* sel, salt, being put instead of

Fig. 6.10. Crisscross lines like those seen on the belt of Offerus.

Scel, seal, which confuses the mind of seekers), the *Mark* and the *Imprint of the Almighty,* his *Signature,* also the *Star of the Magi, the Pole Star,* etc.

Fulcanelli goes on to say,

The secret version of this positive truth in the Epiphany cake, which it is the custom for families to eat at Epiphany, the famous feast marking the manifestation of the Christ Child to the three Magi-Kings and to the gentiles. . . . It is the child Jesus, carried by Offerus, the servant or the Traveller; it is the gold in its bath, the bather; it is the bean, the sabot, the cradle or the cross of honour and it is also the fish "which swims in our philosophic water."

Fulcanelli then likens the fish to the "hieroglyph of the Philosophers' Stone in its first state."[5]

Another clue, found at the website mentioned above, was in the Priestess card in the Tarot deck of Aleister Crowley (fig. 6.11). The Priestess is seen holding a net or veil, which is the "idea behind all form, the veil which hides the Eternal Spirit; and the link between the archetypical and formative worlds." It "represents the influence and means of incarnation."[6] This sounds very similar to the forces of creation moving through the paths of the Tree of Life.

Fig. 6.11. The Priestess, from
Aleister Crowley's Tarot deck

Until this point I hadn't noticed that the Tree of Life has not just one but three veils, which are commonly referred to as the Three Veils of Negative Existence. They are named Ain, Ain Soph, and Ain Soph Aur. *Ain* literally means *nothing; Ain Soph* means *no limit,* hence *the boundless* or *infinite; Ain Soph Aur* means *boundless light.*

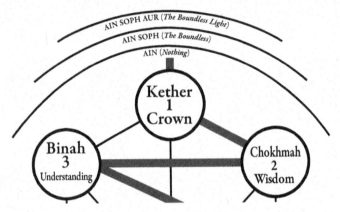

Fig. 6.12. Three Veils of Negative Existence over the Tree of Life

The three veils, in the form of the grid of templates, are used to cover the Tree of Life. Three veils, forming one large covering, serve as a boundary between the physical world and the spiritual world. Three in one, much like the Holy Trinity in Christianity and like trinities in various other religions. The dimensions of the components of the template are symbolic of the heavens, with the precession of the equinoxes, the sun, Venus, and the moon. Like the two outside pillars of the Tree of Life, they represent masculine and feminine attributes. When viewed in their entirety on a map, the templates form the crisscross design mentioned by Fulcanelli in his explanation of the crisscross symbol on the belt of Offerus. Its interpretations refer to the Seal of God, the Star of the Magi, the mark and imprint of the Almighty, the cross of honor, and the fish that swims in the hieroglyph of the Philosophers' Stone. The pillars of Boaz and Jachin are represented in both the Tree of Life and the templates.

Not only do the three veils represent the foundations that support various religious beliefs, but they also represent sciences such as mathematics and astronomy, which connect with alchemy and Kabbalah.

In addition to the large Veil template, if we count the locations of the medium and small templates, we are presented with a total of 3,003 possible locations.

The large template consists of 33 locations.

The center and 8 of the outside locations contain a medium template, for a total of 9 additional templates, each of which has 33 locations, adding 297 additional locations.

$$9 \times 33 = 297$$

Each of the medium templates contain 9 small templates, each of which also contains 33 locations, presenting us with 2,673 more locations.

$$9 \times 9 \times 33 = 2,673$$

33 (large template locations) + 297 (medium template locations) + 2,673 (small template locations) = 3,003 locations

I find it interesting that each step holds the number 33 (33 + 297 = 330, and 330 + 2,673 = 3,003). Ninety-one templates with 33 locations in each, for a total of 3,003 locations. It sounds unreal. How could anyone possibly have enough treasure to bury in each of those locations? Add to that the fact that this only makes up one large cell of the entire Veil or grid of cells that covers much of North America, and it sounds extremely unrealistic. I don't believe each of these locations contains a treasure. Many of them do, but not all of them. Those locations on the template that don't contain any treasures are, in my opinion, serving a symbolic role.

Every number involved in this has a meaning. When we finally get a grasp on the meanings of scales, dimensions, symbols, and numbers involved in this template, we can get a much clearer view of the story behind it all. Even the number 91 (the total number of templates in each large template) has a meaning behind it, and it ties in with the other symbols. (Remember, a single large template contains 9 medium templates, with 8 being located on its outer edges and 1 located in the center. Each medium template contains 9 small templates, 8 on its outer edges and 1 in the center. This gives us 1 large template, 9 medium templates, and 81 small templates, for a total of 91 templates.) The number 91 is the gematria for the Hebrew word *amen* but also for the Rabbinic Hebrew word for *tree,* which is 'ilan' (אילן). It is also the triangle of the number 13, meaning that it is the sum of integers from 1 to 13.

I felt satisfied with the interpretations regarding the Tree of Life and Veil templates. The fact that both templates work together shows that they predate the Knights of the Golden Circle. The numbers involved with both templates and the symbolism strongly suggest that they fall in line with Freemason and Rosicrucian ideologies. I believed that the Veil template was not a KGC Template, but a Freemasonic and Rosicrucian invention, and I also felt certain that it was Francis Bacon and his peers that put all this together. They had great influence on Freemasonry and Rosicrucianism, and through those organizations their ideas grew into a secret reality. I thought I had it all figured out, until an illustration in a small book from the early sixteenth century put a dent in my theory.

7   GATES OF LIGHT

In 1516, a man by the name of Paolo Riccio, also known as Paulus Riccius, published a book titled *Portae Lucis*, which translates into English as *Gates of Light*. The illustration on the frontispiece of this book is said to be the first time that a diagram of the Tree of Life was reproduced for a public audience (see fig. 7.1, page 62). The book is a translation of a work by Rabbi Joseph ben Abraham Gikatilla (1248–ca. 1325) and can currently be viewed online at Austrian Literature Online, a website operated by the University of Innsbruck, Austria.

Paolo Riccio was a Jewish convert to Catholicism, a student of Christian Kabbalah, and a professor at the University of Pavia in Italy, and he served as physician to the Holy Roman Emperor Maximilian I. "Riccio relates that he was ordered by Emperor Maximilian to prepare a Latin translation of the Talmud. All that has come down of it are the translations of the tractates Berakot, Sanhedrin, and Makkot (Augsburg, 1519), which are the earliest Latin renderings of the Mishnah known to bibliographers."[1]

The fact that a Tree of Life was published prior to the birth of Francis Bacon was not an issue; on its own, that would have had no effect on my theory. What did affect some portions of my theory were parts of the illustration surrounding the Tree of Life. The illustration contains several symbols and includes what I believe could be a map.

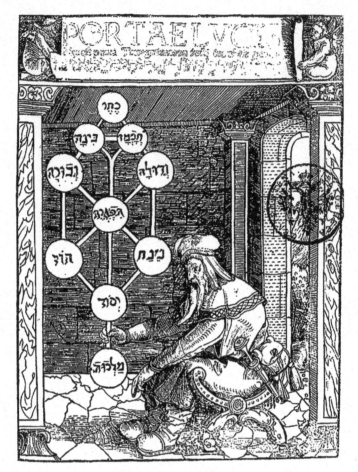

Fig. 7.1. The frontispiece of *Portae Lucis*, 1516.

Apart from the Tree of Life in the illustration above, which is a lit-tle different in shape than most Trees seen today, I immediately noticed the crisscross design of what I have come to refer to as the Veil. The man is most likely a Jewish rabbi and appears to be wearing heavy boots, gloves, and a pack, and is armed with a short sword or dagger. Since the book is a translation of a work by Gikatilla, I would assume that the man in the illustration would be Gikatilla himself. He is dressed for traveling, which could possibly serve as a symbol for traveling the spiritual path of the Tree of Life. The hashmarks on the wall behind the man could very well be a representation of rain, which is often seen as a blessing. (I might not have pieced together the rain symbolism in the *Portae Lucis* map without the modern music video titled "Victoria Hanna–The Aleph-bet song (Hosha'ana)" on YouTube.)

The man in the illustration is pointing at his boots. Directly in front of his boots appear to be ripples in water, as if he is on one side, facing in the direction of the water, and on the other side of the water are more tiles. The shape of the tiles on the other side of the ripples looked vaguely familiar to me. I had a hunch, so I searched for a sixteenth-century world map and overlaid it on the illustration from *Portae Lucis*. To say that

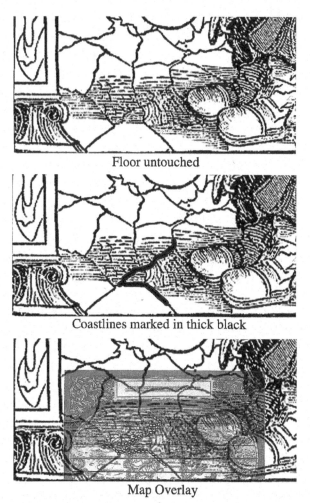

Floor untouched

Coastlines marked in thick black

Map Overlay

Fig. 7.2. Hidden map in illustration from *Portae Lucis*

I was amazed was an understatement. When I overlaid the illustration with a map from 1544, the area below the Tree of Life on the drawing matched the shape of the Atlantic Ocean and the eastern coastline of the United States, as well as the coastlines of Mexico, Central America, and parts of South America! It isn't perfect, but it is very close, and it is certainly close enough to convey a message.

Fig. 7.3. World map published by German cartographer
Sebastian Munster in 1544

Now this could mean a couple of things. It could fall in line with the Tree of Life template I had discovered, and if that was the case, it wasn't Francis Bacon and his peers who came up with the Tree of Life template, but someone before them. It could also mean the New World offered opportunities for people, including Jews, who for centuries had

suffered under inquisitions, discrimination, and harassment throughout Europe. It could have held out a branch of hope for those living an
almost hellish, uncertain life in Europe. There are no words that come
close to describing the horrors they went through. As Edward Kritzler
describes in his book *Jewish Pirates of the Caribbean:* "When Spain's
Monarchs banished the Jews to purify their nation, followers of the Law
of Moses sailed with the explorers and marched with the conquistadors.
With the discovery and settlement of the New World, they took solace
in the hope of finding a safe haven, or at least putting distance between
themselves and the Inquisition."[2]

Everything about that illustration can be viewed as relating to the
Tree of Life template, but on the same note, everything about that illustration can be viewed as relating to Jews looking for a safe haven. There
is, however, one more symbol in this illustration that tips the scales in
favor of the Tree of Life template. That symbol comes in the form of
what forensic geologist, author, and host of the History Channel's H2
program *America Unearthed* Scott Wolter has described as a hooked X
symbol. In the illustration from *Portae Lucis,* the X is the chair the
man is seated on, and his short sword or dagger serves as the hook (see
fig. 7.4). If this is indeed a hooked X symbol, then that could tie the
treasure of the Veil and Tree of Life to the Knights Templar. In fact, the
Veil template marks a location very near the site where the Kensington
Runestone was discovered.

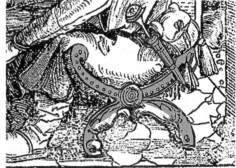

Fig. 7.4. The hooked X symbol on the drawing from *Portae Lucis*

The Kensington Runestone, discovered near Kensington, Minnesota, has been a topic of debate since the time it was discovered in 1898. Some claim it is a hoax, while others have gone through great lengths to show that it is indeed legitimate. On the stone can be found ancient runes, among which is a hooked X symbol. This hooked X symbol got Scott Wolter started on his trail of discoveries: he wanted to know if the stone was a hoax or if it was authentic. After determining the stone's authenticity, he went on to several other discoveries, linking the hooked X symbol to Christopher Columbus, the St. Clair family of Rosslyn Chapel in Scotland, and the Knights Templar.

Now we have more puzzling questions. If this does have some kind of Templar connection, why would Paolo Riccio, a Jewish convert to Catholicism, have anything to do with it, especially two hundred years after the Templars were destroyed by a deeply indebted king of France and the Catholic church?

In searching for answers, I decided to start from yet another angle. The first template I worked with, the Veil template, has a unique shape. I had already gone over the numbers and shape of that template, interpreting the circle and square as a joining of the Heavens and Earth, male and female, but I wanted to take another look at it in regard to religious structures. What did I know about the Templars and Jews other than that they had been treated with extreme prejudice by the Catholic church? What, if anything, stood out in regard to religion or religious structures? Could I find anything that would connect or tie in with the Veil template? After much more research, I finally found an answer, or at least a very good clue.

The first temple in Jerusalem was on the Temple Mount, and on the Temple Mount today is the Dome of the Rock and the Al-Aqsa Mosque. Looking at the design of the Veil template or an individual cell of the template, I found its design was almost identical to the design of the Dome of the Rock (see fig. 7.5).

I found a nice diagram of the layout of the Dome of the Rock in a book by W. R. Lethaby titled *Architecture, Mysticism, and Myth,*

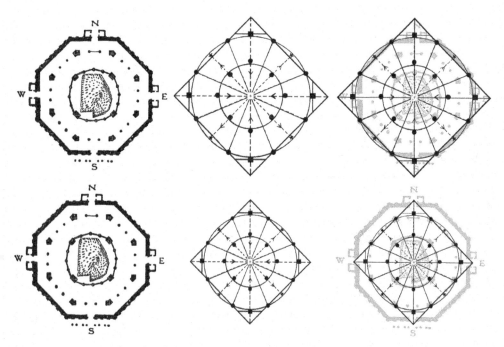

Fig. 7.5. Dome of the Rock with Template overlay

published in 1892. I added the template and then the Dome of the Rock layout, with an overlay of the template. I first lined up the template with the outer edges of the octagonal walls of the Dome of the Rock, but the fit wasn't quite right; however, as you can see on my second attempt from left to right across the bottom of the illustration, the inner and outer circles match the inner and outer circles within the confines of the Dome of the Rock.

One thing I found wrong with Lethaby's illustration was in the compass bearings he used. The Dome of the Rock isn't oriented like that, and neither is the large Veil template; they are both turned a few degrees west of north, that is, counterclockwise, which is referred to as the "occult pole" by some. Figure 7.6 on page 68 gives a better description of the actual orientation.

If the Templars were involved in the Tree of Life and Veil templates, why pattern the template after the Dome of the Rock in Jerusalem? The Knights Templar were there, and they, like many Jews, Christians, and

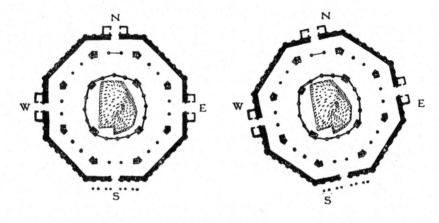

Fig. 7.6. Dome of the Rock: Lethaby's diagram is on the left;
the actual orientation of the Dome is on the right.

Muslims today, considered it one of the holiest sites in the world: "The Knights Templar, active from c. 1119, identified the Dome of the Rock as the site of the Temple of Solomon and set up their headquarters in the Al-Aqsa Mosque adjacent to the Dome for much of the 12th century. The Templum Domini, as they called the Dome of the Rock, featured on the official seals of the Order's Grand Masters (such as Everard des Barres and Renaud de Vichiers), and soon became the model for round Templar churches across Europe."[3]

One of the best-known round Templar churches is the Temple Church in London, built by the Templars in 1186. It's a beautiful building, full of history, but what really caught my eye was a design on a door on its western side (see fig. 7.7).

It's not an exact match, but it is very close. Instead of a square, the Temple Church design is a diamond shape (rhombus), and the inner circle isn't visible unless we use a little imagination and notice that the scroll-work on the inside hints at the presence of the inner circle. This is very similar to the template and fits the scale. Like most symbols, it could convey a message to those in the know without giving away the secret.

We have the Veil template matching the design of the Dome of the Rock, and it also matches well with a design on the door of a Templar

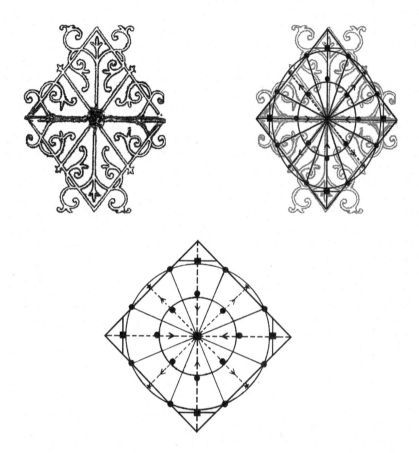

Fig. 7.7. Design from a door of the Temple Church (top left) with template overlay (top right). The template itself is at the bottom.

church. We have the Tree of Life from the frontispiece of an early sixteenth-century book in conjunction with a hidden map of the New World, and a hooked X symbol, which has been traced to the Knights Templar by forensic geologist Scott Wolter. But we need more.

What I did not have at the time were the names of people showing a line of succession back to known Knights Templar.

8 LINE OF SUCCESSION

I find myself starting again at the beginning, with my late mother, Betty Dorsett Duke. She is the reason I got involved in this in the first place: when she brought the truth about Jesse James to light, she opened doors we never knew existed. Had it not been for her, I probably would have never heard of the Knights of the Golden Circle and the treasure legends attributed to them. I would never have looked beyond them and found that stories of their involvement in these treasures are most likely a false trail, leading away from the narrow and rocky path to truth. Through all the years of research, I have continually found myself coming back to the beginning, and each time I return with a little more knowledge than I had before. Running forth, returning, and starting off again with a slightly different view than before.

My objective in this chapter is to show a line of succession tying my research back to the Knights Templar. In previous chapters I have covered connections from where I began my search. I took it back to Williamsburg, Virginia, and further back to Francis Bacon. There are also many other names that could be added to this list, and others who will very likely remain unnamed, but my goal in this chapter is to show a connection between those I have already named and the Knights Templar.

Three names I think are important to start with for the purposes of this chapter are Thomas Jefferson, George Washington, and Benjamin Franklin. All three were Freemasons. Washington and Jefferson both had ties to the College of William and Mary and were among several Founding Fathers who attended services at the Bruton Parish Church. "A 17-year-old George Washington received his surveyor's license through W&M and would return as its first American chancellor. Thomas Jefferson received his undergraduate education here, as did presidents John Tyler and James Monroe."[1] As for Jefferson, author and Freemason Timothy Hogan writes, "Some would dispute Jefferson's involvement in Freemasonry since initiation records no longer survive for him, however the record of him being present at several public Masonic events, his appointing several well-known Masons to top level posts, the fact that a Masonic code cipher was found among his personal papers, he was known to have marched in Masonic processions, he attended cornerstone laying ceremonies, two Grand Lodges held funeral processions for him after his death, and his son-in-law Governor of Virginia Thomas M. Randolph, his favorite grandson Thomas Jefferson Randolph, and his nephews Peter and Samuel Carr were all members of Door to Virtue Lodge No. 44, Albemarle County, Virginia, should all attest to the fact that he had more than just a side interest in the fraternity."[2] Jefferson's mentor, Professor William Small at the College of William and Mary, taught natural philosophy and mathematics and was a student of the Enlightenment, following in the footsteps of Francis Bacon and Isaac Newton.

In searching for Franklin's ties with the College of William and Mary, I found that "the College of William and Mary was instrumental in opening a school in 1760, at the urging of Benjamin Franklin, no less and so became the first college in America involved in the education of black students."[3] Benjamin Franklin was a Fellow of the Royal Society and a staunch Baconian. The website for the Rosicrucian order AMORC states that "Benjamin Franklin, Thomas Jefferson and Thomas Paine were intimately connected with the Rosicrucian community."[4] Franklin was also accepted into Masonic lodges and academic societies in France, where he found support that was crucial in gaining American independence. One of the early influences on Franklin's scientific interests came from Harvard professor John Winthrop. Professor Winthrop's great-uncle was John Winthrop Jr., governor of Connecticut.

Before coming to New England and being appointed governor of Connecticut in 1631, Winthrop, while studying law and Christian alchemy in London, had developed an interest in Rosicrucianism and later became a member of the Royal Society. Winthrop "began to display a special affinity for the English alchemist John Dee. Dee, whose mystical approach to experimental science has been linked by historians to both the origins of the Rosicrucian movement and the Arabic works of Avicenna (Ibn Sina) and Artephius, had a special interest in scientific exploration of the New World." John Dee had ideas of forming a colony in the New World "which he intended to call Atlantis."[5] Dee, a well-known occult philosopher, is said by many highly esteemed Francis Bacon researchers to have served as a mentor to the young Bacon.

The fact that Winthrop, the colonial governor of Connecticut, was involved with Rosicrucianism, Christian alchemy, and the Royal Society (formed by well-known Baconians) and had a deep interest in the works of John Dee would place him among possible New World contacts for fostering Bacon's New Atlantis and helping to bring it into reality.

Like Winthrop, Isaac Newton, one of the most influential scientists in history, was one of the earliest Fellows of the Royal Society and later became its president. Newton was also an alchemist and a Rosicrucian; his friend and associate Christopher Wren was also a member of the Royal Society. It is said that Newton highly regarded the scientific work of Christopher Wren. As I have mentioned earlier in this book, Christopher Wren probably was a Freemason as well.

It's clear that the men mentioned above had ties to one another, either through Freemasonry, Rosicrucianism, or both. They were students of alchemy, mathematics, natural philosophy, and more. Some suggest the Royal Society served as an informal Masonic lodge where, because of the climate of the times, they could safely meet and share their findings and ideas. Had these men voiced some of their views publicly, the church would have had them condemned and put pressure on the rulers of the day to punish them as heretics. These highly educated, goal-oriented men weren't the type to waste time pondering the meaning of life, but instead put their ideas into motion. Adherents of and successors to Francis Bacon, they carried the idea of New Atlantis into reality. They weren't the only men involved, however: the dream they brought to reality required the efforts and solidarity of many men from various walks of life. As Manly Palmer Hall suggested, this undertaking took the efforts of secret societies throughout the Western world to complete. It wasn't just the ideas of one man or one group, but many, with the same dreams of liberty and freedom from political and religious tyranny.

One man more than any other is credited with helping to form the mind of the young Francis Bacon. That man is John Dee, the original 007. Dee was a man of many talents; in addition to serving as advisor to Queen Elizabeth I, he was an alchemist, mathematician, occult philosopher, astrologer, and spy. He would often sign letters to the queen as 007. Dee studied with and was friends with Gerolamo Cardano, an Italian philosopher, mathematician, astronomer, and physician. Gerolamo's father, Fazio Cardano, was a mathematician and devotee of Hermetic science and the occult. Fazio was friends with Leonardo da Vinci, who was in turn a student of John Argyropoulos, a philosopher, teacher, and writer who is credited with bringing the classical literature and philosophy of the ancient Greeks to Western Europe.

Another student of John Argyropoulos was Johann Reuchlin. Reuchlin, born in Germany, was a humanist, Greek and Hebrew scholar, philosopher, and author of several books. At a time when the Catholic church was attacking the Jews, Reuchlin stood in defense of Jewish literature and championed religious toleration in the face of the Inquisition. This resulted in a papal verdict against Reuchlin, ordering him to be silent. Reuchlin became interested in the Kabbalah after meeting another student of Argyropoulos, Giovanni Pico della Mirandola. In 1517, Reuchlin published a book, *De arte cabalistica* (On the Kabbalistic art), in which he covers Messianism, Pythagoreanism, and Kabbalah. In composing this book, he used materials sent to him by Jerome Riccio, the son of Paolo Riccio, who published the Latin translation of Gikatilla's *Portae Lucis*. As mentioned in chapter 7, Paolo Riccio also served as physician and counselor to Emperor Maximilian I, who was apparently on friendly terms with Freemasons, who were at that time said to have been actual stonemasons.

In *The History of Freemasonry*, Albert Gallatin Mackey includes the following extract from the writings of a cardinal archbishop of Westminster:

> The south of France, where a large Jewish and Saracenic element remained, was a hotbed of heresies, and that region was also a favorite one with the guild of Masons. It is asserted too that, as far back as the 12th century, the lodges of the guild enjoyed the special protection of the Knights Templars. It is easy in this way to understand how the symbolical allusion to Solomon and his Temple might have passed from the Knights into the Masonic formulary. In this way too might be explained how after the suppression of the Order of the Temple, some of the recalcitrant, maintaining their influence over the Freemasons, would be able to prevent what had been hitherto a harmless ceremony into an elaborate ritual that should impart some of the errors of the Templars to the initiated. A document was long ago published, which purports to be a charter granted to a lodge of Freemasons in England, in the time of Henry VII., and it bears the marks in its religious indifference of a suspicious likeness between Freemasons of then and now. In Germany, the guild was numerous and was formally recognized by a diploma granted in 1489 by the Emperor Maximilian. But this sanction was finally revoked by the Imperial Diet in 1707.[6]

Paolo Riccio's brother, Augustinus Riccius (Riccio), was a follower of Abraham Zacuto, a Sephardic Jew, historian, astronomer, and rabbi who knew Cornelius Agrippa and was the royal astronomer for King John II of Portugal. Christopher Columbus used Zacuto's astronomic tables on his famous trip to the New World, and when looking for funding for that trip, Columbus met with King John II. Columbus's request for funding was denied—though some believe Columbus remained loyal to King John II—so he turned to King Ferdinand and Queen Isabella of Spain. Upon his return from discovering the New World, Columbus announced his discovery to King John II, who replied that Columbus's discovery was also under the influence of Portugal. Before Columbus could get word to King Ferdinand and Queen Isabella, King John had contacted them, and in the end, he got a cut of the discoveries. There is evidence enough to cause suspicion, leaving some researchers wondering if Columbus was working for King John II the entire time. If so, the king had a shrewd business plan in that Spain would finance the exploration, and if or when it paid off, Portugal could draw the water from the well which Spain had dug.

Columbus himself is said by many to have been a member of the Knights of Christ, while others say he was closely associated with them and that his father-in-law was a member of the order. The Knights of Christ were a modification of the Knights Templar, and King John II is said by some to have been the order's grand master at that time. "In Portugal, the Order was cleared by an inquiry and simply modified its name, becoming Knights of Christ. Under this title, they functioned well into the sixteenth century, devoting themselves to maritime activity. Vasco da Gama was a Knight of Christ, and Prince Henry the Navigator was a Grand Master of the Order. Ships of the Knights of Christ sailed under the familiar red pattée cross. And it was under the same cross that Christopher Columbus's three caravels crossed the Atlantic to the New World. Columbus himself was married to the daughter of a former Knight of Christ, and had access to his father-in-law's charts and diaries."[7]

Societies such as these often had similar goals and interests. Among the interests shared by various societies, scholars, alchemists, artists, and others was the need for an outlet where they could express their ideas without fear of persecution. Among those individuals was Abraham Gikatilla, author of the *Portae Lucis*. He was a Kabbalist and a student of Abraham Abulafia, a Spanish Jewish mystic and founder of the school of prophetic Kabbalah. Abulafia's dream was for Christians, Jews, and Muslims to unite through the beliefs they had in common, which some researchers believe is one of the secret goals held by those who founded the Knights Templar. Abulafia wrote to Pope Nicholas III, announcing his intention to come to Rome to convert the pope. The pope responded by ordering his men to burn Abraham Abulafia at the stake as soon as he arrived in the city. Luckily for Abraham, the pope had a stroke and died the night before Abraham arrived; he was jailed for a short time and then released.

Abraham was the nephew of Meir Abulafia, who often corresponded with and was friendly with Rabbi Samson ben Abraham of Sens; although the two quarreled later, Meir spoke of Samson's father, Abraham, "as a pious, saintly, and noble man."[8]

Samson was a great-grandson of Rabbi Solomon ben Isaac, also known as Rashi, who was a favored court guest of Hugh (or Hugues), Count of Champagne, one of the most important figures involved in the formation of the Knights Templar. Author Karen Ralls states that the court of Hugh was "known to have been a haven for Jews and other non-Catholics who fled persecution. Rabbi Rashi started his famed Kabbalistic school, also based at Troyes, in 1070. He was renowned for his expert translation skills and especially adept at translating Hebrew into other languages, including French. St. Bernard, the Cistercian abbot of Clairvaux, as well as abbots from other Orders, highly valued the skills of certain learned scholars in Champagne (and elsewhere) who were well versed in Hebrew, Greek, Latin and Aramaic, some of whom stayed at various abbeys for long periods of time translating texts."[9] In addition, Timothy Hogan says in his book

The Way of the Templar, "Rashi had been initiated into the Rose Cross Order established by Amus, and was one of the leading lights within it. Rashi was born in Troyes and he in fact likewise secretly initiated Godfrey de Bouillon into this tradition, and had originally entrusted in him certain secrets regarding artifacts in the Holy Land. Rashi had also been an early tutor of Saint Bernard of Clairvaux, who wrote the first Rule for the Templar Order. In fact, this is why the first Templar Rule was 72 articles, which corresponded to the 72 Qabbalistic names of God."[10]

Those mentioned above are but a few of the great people involved throughout the centuries in building a great work—a nation free of tyranny and oppression from heads of state and powerful religious figures. Many had the common trait of having been persecuted for views or beliefs that differed from the established powers of their day. Some kings were lenient, as were some religious leaders, but there was little stability in that; when one leader passed away, he was oftentimes replaced with a holy terror. The New Atlantis was a beautiful dream, formed in large part by the oppression all these figures had suffered. Through the efforts of Jewish and Christian Kabbalists and adherents of various other religious faiths, along with secret orders such as the Knights Templar, Freemasons, and Rosicrucians, this dream has been, and continues to be, formed into a reality.

The people listed above show a clear line of succession from the founding of the Knights Templar through the Middle Ages into the Age of Discovery and to the founding of America, where they buried treasures using the Tree of Life and Veil templates.

Why did they do this, and what exactly did they bury? We know of treasures consisting of gold and jewels in Victorio Peak, New Mexico and in Georgetown, Texas, and we know of the gold buried by Jesse James aka James L. Courtney and a young George Roming in Bell County, Texas. We also know of Marie Bauer Hall's writings concerning the Bruton Vault stating that its treasure may contain documents and records of great importance. But what kind of documents and items could possibly be so important that secret societies would have gone through so much trouble over the centuries to keep them hidden? The answer to that could lie in a mystery you've most likely already heard about, and one of the clues just might be found in a famous work of art.

9 ARCADIAN SHEPHERDS

The famous work of art by Nicolas Poussin known as *Et in Arcadia ego,* also known as *The Arcadian Shepherds,* portrays shepherds gathered around an ancient tomb in a peaceful and beautiful setting (see fig. 9.1, page 80).

The name, subjects, and possible locations in this painting have been at the center of controversy for years. I first heard of it when I read the book *Holy Blood, Holy Grail* by Michael Baigent, Richard Leigh, and Henry Lincoln. The titles *Et in Arcadia ego* and *The Arcadian Shepherds* give two important clues to how this could tie in with the New Atlantis, aka the New World or America.

Et in Arcadia ego can be and is often translated as meaning *I am also in Arcadia,* which raises the question, what and where is Arcadia?

Arcadia is a region of the central Peloponnesus in Greece. Extremely hilly, it was chiefly the home of shepherds and goatherds. As such, it became a setting for pastoral poetry. In mythology, it was presided over by the god Pan. Over the centuries its name became synonymous with pastoral areas, idealized utopias, and a paradise inhabited by spirits of nature and shepherds all living in harmony—a type of Edenic garden. In 1524, the Italian explorer Giovanni da Verrazzano, who sailed along the eastern coast of North America from Virginia to Nova Scotia, called this area Arcadia. At the time of Poussin's painting in 1637–38, it would

Fig. 9.1. *Et in Arcadia* ego by Nicolas Poussin, painted 1637–38

have seemed logical to assume that Arcadia could have easily applied to the eastern coastline of North America ranging from Virginia to Nova Scotia (see fig. 9.2). Author, historian, and philosopher Peter Dawkins[1] states in his essay "The Oak Island Mystery, Part 2: The Navigators" that "allegorically, Arcadia is known as the land of the Rosicrucians—a land inhabited by shepherd-knights and poets, and famous for its harmonious landscapes and oak tree woods in which boars hunt for acorns."[2] In part 3 of Dawkins' Oak Island essay, he says that "for the early 17th century Rosicrucians, Oak Island and the area of Nova Scotia close to it represent both the star Deneb and the cornerstone of the 'new land' of Virginia. The coastal landscape of Virginia corresponds to the main body of Cygnus, the Swan, aka the Northern Cross. It was also known as Arcadia, the Land of the Rosicrucians." Dawkins goes further in stating that "in Baconian terms, this 'virginal' Arcadian land is the earthly counterpart of what could be the beginning of the New Atlantis."[3]

Fig. 9.2. Verrazzano's exploratory voyage of 1524

Dawkins writes of the constellation Cygnus the Swan, or Northern Cross, and how it ties in with Arcadia in the New World, of which Oak Island and its treasure can be considered as being the "cornerstone" (see pages 98–99). In his essay, Dawkins employs the David Rumsey Map Collection, specifically the celestial globe created by Giovanni Maria Cassini, which is described as "a Celestial Globe made in Rome in 1792. It is constructed from 12 engraved globe gores (a gore being a segment of a curved surface). All of the constellations and important stars are shown. The heavens are shown as they would be seen by an observer looking from the center of the earth."[4] While studying the map, I noticed the constellation Lyra, the Lyre, in the heartland of the United States, and it dawned on me that the lyre shares an interesting similarity with *Et in Arcadia ego*.

When viewing Poussin's painting, I noticed that the shadow of the kneeling man in the center being cast onto the tomb is shaped like a harp. At first glance, I thought it was just a shadow, but considering the

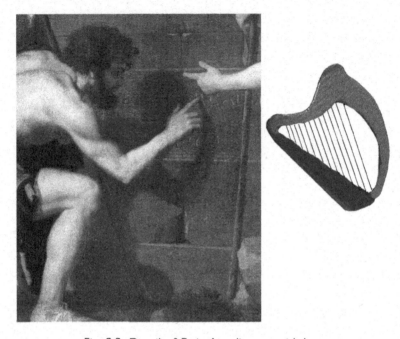

Fig. 9.3. Detail of *Et in Arcadia ego*, with harp

angle of light, it seemed more than just slightly off. The shadow cast from his knee is at a different angle than the shadow of his elbow. The shadow of his knee would suggest the sun is higher in the sky, while the shadow cast by his elbow would suggest the sun is lower, nearer the horizon. The shadow of his forearm is curved. There is no shadow of the staff being held by the man to his right, even though that staff is very close to the tomb, and the upper portion of the staff being held by the man kneeling is also missing its shadow. Poussin was a master artist, which leads me to believe this shadow was no accident and that he could have been using it to convey a message. Some may see this as a wild claim, but this isn't the first time Poussin has been suspected of employing hidden messages. He is known to have encoded messages in some of his works, including the one we're currently discussing. Sandy Hamblett wrote, "Poussin himself said his paintings had a definite and perhaps secret import when he suggested that 'these things (the meaning in his paintings) I believe, will not displease those people who know how to read them.' Art scholar Judith Bernstock said that to 'receive Poussin's paintings . . . one must study them continually and closely, always searching them for connections.' As the great Bernini once said, while pointing to his own head, 'Poussin was an artist who works up here' (i.e., with his brain) and Bernini further asserted that he was 'a great storyteller.' The suggestion that the paintings of Poussin could have a hidden meaning then comes from the mouth of the artist himself. Poussin had indicated that these meanings could be discerned by those who knew how to read them. By this he meant his patrons or others who were able to interpret the canvases, in other words, perhaps those who were initiated."[5]

The harp-shaped shadow in Poussin's painting stayed on the back burner of my mind for several years, until it came to the forefront as I read Dawkins's essay regarding Oak Island, which led me to Cassini's *Celestial Globe*. I created the image you see on page 84 (fig. 9.4), which is very similar to that shown in the *Celestial Globe*. Both Cassini's map and the image on the next page show the constellation Lyra situated over the heartland of the present-day United States. Of the constellation, the ancient Greek astronomer Ptolemy said, "Lyra is like Venus and Mercury,"[6] which in turn correspond to the seventh and eighth sefiroth on the Tree of Life: Mercury is connected with Hod, Splendor, and Venus, Netzach, with Victory. The placement of Lyra over the United States as it is in the map above corresponds with the sefiroth mentioned above in the Tree of Life template I discovered. The seventh sefirah, Netzach and Venus, is near Georgetown, Texas, and the eighth sefirah, Hod and Mercury, is in the western portion of central Kansas. The sixth sefirah, Tiphareth, Beauty, connected to the sun, is in eastern Oklahoma. The ninth sefirah, Yesod, Foundation, connected with the moon, is located on the western side of Lyra in the Texas Panhandle.

The tenth sefirah, Malkuth, Kingdom, connected with the Earth and located at Victorio Peak, rests between Lyra and the right knee of Hercules. On the *Celestial Globe*, there is a four-pointed star very near the location of Victorio Peak. I'm not sure if that star has a name, or

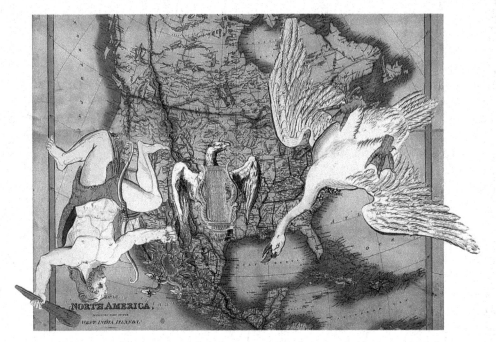

Fig. 9.4. Locations of constellations over North America in 1792

if it even is a star. It could possibly represent the apple branch that, in some maps, Hercules held in his left hand, and which is related to the eleventh labor of Hercules. Hercules is said to be kneeling in prayer to his father, Zeus, represented by an eagle, who, soaring high above, can see everything below, much like Zeus on his throne on Mount Olympus. Zeus represents Kingdom, with Hercules kneeling before him. Note that in *Et in Arcadia ego,* the man in the center pointing at the lyre-shaped shadow is kneeling just as Hercules is depicted in the constellation maps.

The Tree of Life has a connection with this as well. Both the Tree of Life and the Tree of Knowledge of Good and Evil were in the Garden of Eden, from which Adam and Eve were expelled and which was guarded by an angel bearing a fiery sword. Most religions have beliefs similar to the biblical story. The Norse have the World Tree Ygdrassil; the Ṭūbā tree in Islamic tradition is a tree of paradise; and the Buddha had his Bodhi tree, under which he gained enlightenment.

Hercules has connections with a similar tree. In his eleventh labor, Hercules was given the task of stealing a golden apple from the Garden of the Hesperides, which was guarded by a multiheaded serpent. These apples offered those who ate them the gift of immortality. Hercules kneels before Zeus, who can be viewed as representing Kingdom, just as the tenth sefirah does; Hercules steals an apple from a tree in a protected garden, much like the Garden of Eden, and the apple is said to offer immortality, just as the fruit from the Tree of Life is said to do—all this seems too much to be mere coincidence. Another point is that Hercules stealing the apples from the garden involves his eleventh labor, and while the Tree of Life has ten sefiroth, it also has an additional hidden one said to be interchangeable with Kether (Crown) which, when counted in, makes eleven.

Lyra, in Greek mythology, was the lyre of Orpheus, said to be the first lyre in history, which was made from a turtle shell. When Orpheus was born to the Thracian King Oeagrus, Apollo presented the lyre as a gift to him. The music made by Orpheus was said to be so great that it charmed both the gods and nature and even silenced the lethal Sirens, who tried to lure Jason and his Argonauts into a watery death while they were searching for the Golden Fleece.

Orpheus's wife was Eurydice. On their wedding day, she was bitten by a snake and died, leaving Orpheus so grief-stricken that the music he played on his lyre made even the gods weep. Orpheus gained entrance to the underworld, where his music charmed Hades, who agreed to let Eurydice travel back to the land of the living on the condition that Orpheus did not look back until he was out of the underworld. He almost made it, but at the last moment he looked back, only to watch his beloved wife falling back into the underworld. Not long after his failure, Orpheus was killed by Thracian Maenads for dishonoring Dionysus, and his lyre was thrown into a river. Zeus is said to have sent an eagle or vulture to retrieve it. He placed it in the sky to become the constellation Lyra. Some legends have it that Orpheus was placed near Lyra and became the constellation Cygnus the Swan.

The brightest star in the constellation of Lyra is Vega, whose "name is derived from the Arabic *Al Nasr al Waki,* the Swooping Eagle, because it is depicted as an eagle, vulture, or falcon bearing a harp or lyre in its talons. In Babylonia it was Dilgan, the Messenger of Light. Pliny called it the Harp Star, in reference to the seven-stringed lyre of Hermes and later Orpheus. Vega is also associated with Apollo, Mercury, King Arthur, and the Biblical King David."[7] The seven strings of Hermes's and Orpheus's lyre correspond with the seven sefiroth in the lower world of the Tree of Life.

Lyra's associations with King Arthur's harp brings to mind Arthur's Round Table, which resonates with the twelve constellations and their precession around the sun, which ties in with the Veil template. The harp association also evokes the Grail romances, which in turn bring to mind the stories of Rennes-le-Château, Rosslyn Chapel, the Knights Templar, and even Jesus and Mary Magdalene. The man who is said to have introduced the Grail and Lancelot to the King Arthur story was Chrétien de Troyes, a French poet from Troyes, France, where the Knight Templar are said to have been founded.

Viewed in the light of the information above, *Et in Arcadia ego* could easily be viewed as pointing to Arcadia located in North America. This doesn't take away from the mystery of Rennes-le-Château by any means (see page 94), and I believe there is still much to be discovered there, but there is just as much if not more to be discovered in North America. The symbols used by Poussin, like most symbols, are rich with meaning, and this ambiguity is part of the beauty of symbolism. As Albert Pike stated, "The symbols of the wise always become the idols of the ignorant multitude."[8] This quote is often used by the closed-minded to bash both Pike and Freemasonry. (In my opinion, this only serves to illuminate their ignorance.) Symbols often have dual meanings, and some have multiple meanings—such as the constellation Lyra, and not just the lyre but also the eagle sent by Zeus to retrieve it. The eagle in turn serves as a symbol of Zeus, to whom his son Hercules kneels in a prayer for assistance. Because Zeus can be viewed as representing Kingdom, the eagle can be associated with the same. Pointing to Arcadia in one place doesn't mean it can't be in another; perhaps it was once in one place and later moved to another, more suitable, and safer environment, such as North America.

A place such as Arcadia, the land of the Rosicrucians, Bacon's New Atlantis, connects the Tree of Life, the Dome of the Rock, the Earth, and the constellations representing the foundation of the United States. The Veil and Tree of Life templates, Poussin's painting, the New Atlantis, and the Greek myths all incorporate aspects of male, female, and Deity, the path leading to the unification of the temporal with the spiritual. This would be used to set a foundation stone for a nation that was to become a beacon of light to the world, ushering in a new Golden Age, a work unfinished. As John Winthrop Sr., father of John Winthrop Jr., said to his fellow Massachusetts Bay colonists when they reached the New World in 1630, "We shall be as a city upon a hill, the eyes of all people are upon us," paraphrasing Jesus, who said, "Ye are the light of the world. A city that is set on a hill cannot be hid" (Matthew 5:4).

10 INTO THE SHADOWS

The information in the previous chapters points to treasures hidden over the years by people associated with the Freemasons, Rosicrucians, and possibly the Knights Templar. Those who buried these treasures employed codes involving Kabbalah, gematria, alchemy, astronomy, Greek mythology, cartography, and art. The idea that these people would place treasure across an entire continent using such an elaborate map, which would have taken decades if not longer to lay out, and that they would bury such a large amount of treasure, is bewildering. Yet that is exactly what they did. We started with my mother, Betty Dorsett Duke, and a treasure map written by her great-grandfather, Jesse James. Living a peaceful, law-abiding life in Texas under the alias of James Lafayette Courtney, he was a Freemason. We read how he and other Freemasons, including George Roming, buried a large treasure in central Texas. From there we traveled back in time, through a line of Freemasons linking the Founding Fathers of the United States to the Bruton Parish Church and the College of William and Mary. These in turn are linked to Freemasons, the Royal Society, Rosicrucians, and Francis Bacon. We went even further, past Francis Bacon, John Dee, and Nicolas Poussin, through Christopher Columbus and some of history's most famous Christian Kabbalists, philosophers, and artists, as well as Jewish rabbis, all the way back to the Knights Templar. We now have a good grasp of who was involved. The question now is, what did they bury? I seriously doubt that they would have gone through all that trouble just to bury gold, silver, and gems. As mentioned earlier, Marie Bauer Hall claimed there are documents of great importance buried in the Bruton Vault. But what about the other sites? What is buried there, and what on earth could possibly be so important?

The answers to this question require us to delve deeper into the Knights Templar and their founding, mission, and fate after their downfall in the early fourteenth century. Poussin and *Et in Arcadia ego* are not only associated with the treasure legends connected with the Tree of Life and Veil templates I discovered, but also with treasure legends around Rennes-le-Château in southern France—a treasure in which the Knights Templar are said to have played a crucial role.

In more recent history, the Knights Templar are often spoken of in the same breath as the Holy Grail, of which there are countless descriptions. In fact, the West doesn't hold a monopoly on the Grail, as many other cultures around the world have similar legends. In *The Alchemical Keys to Masonic Ritual,* Timothy Hogan writes:

> The science of alchemy is quite ancient. Not only is it found in some of the oldest Egyptian texts, but we find it in the oldest Sumerian texts as well. In fact, the alchemical science in Sumer was called "GRA.AL," and this is almost unquestionably the origin of the Holy Graal—or "Grail" tradition. (This ancient history is covered extensively in the book *Revelation of the Holy Grail* by Chevalier Emerys). Alchemy was then fundamental to the institutions and philosophical schools of ancient Greece, and its doctrines were passed on by philosophers like Pythagoras, Plato, Socrates and Aristotle. It was later propagated by the Essenes, early Muslims, Jewish Qabbalists and the Knights Templar and cathedral builders in Europe. Finally, we also see it as the corner

stone in the works of people like Francis Bacon, Isaac Newton, Robert Boyle, Elias Ashmole and others who developed the Royal Society of Britain.[1]

This quote confirms what I have said in previous chapters—evidence pointing at a connection between Freemasonry and the Knights Templar. Hogan goes on to discuss the two prominent schools of thought concerning Freemasonry and its origins, one saying that they came from the cathedral builders, the other saying that they came from the Knights Templar. He writes, "Whether we are looking at cathedral builders or Orders of Knighthood as Freemasonry's origins, both theories lead to the same source—the Knights Templar."[2]

As the story goes, after the first crusades, in which Jerusalem was captured, people throughout Europe made pilgrimages to the Holy Land. These pilgrims were often robbed and killed for their valuables, creating a need for protection. This led to the founding of the Knights Templar, an order originally made up of nine poor knights. One of the largest problems with that story is trying to figure out how nine poor knights were to go about filling such a need. How do nine men protect pilgrims from legions of bandits in the Middle East? It doesn't make sense, but the fact remains: this order was started by nine knights, all related, some by blood, some by marriage, and they were set up in the Al-Aqsa Mosque on the Temple Mount, which was believed to have been the former site of Solomon's Temple. How do nine poor knights in a newly formed order acquire such prestigious and holy accommodations? In a National Geographic documentary titled *Templars' Lost Treasure,* author Karen Ralls says that the knights "presented themselves to King Baldwin II, the king of Jerusalem at the time, and they were given what we might call today five-star accommodation on the southeastern platform of the Temple Mount."[3]

There had to have been a lot of activity going on behind the

Fig. 10.1. *Sangreal*, illustration by Arthur Rackham, 1917.
Notice the crisscross design in the windows,
reminiscent of the belt of Offerus
(shown in figure 6.10).

scenes. We know that the founding members of the Knights Templar included Hugh, Count of Champagne, and that among his favored court guests was the famous Rabbi Rashi, who is said to have been a descendant of King David, the father of King Solomon. According to the legend, from Rashi and others the Templars gained some knowledge of hidden treasures on the Temple Mount. As soon as they gained possession of the site, they began digging. They are said to have already known exactly where to dig, and after a short time, they found the treasures they were looking for. Once they found them, they rushed back to France and in short order went from nine poor knights to the wealthiest order in Christendom; researchers claim at their peak they numbered in the tens of thousands. According to Timothy Hogan, the Templars knew that another crusade was coming and wanted to safeguard not only the sacred items of Judaism, but also items and documents held sacred by other religions in that part of the world. In an interview, Hogan explains:

> There were certain families that perpetuated gnostic Christian thought and who were in association with some of the Kabbalists in Troyes in France and also in Spain, and who were also in contact with some of the Sufi and Druze traditions. There was a mission that was put forward in order to try to get these mystical traditions to all come in contact and work together in order to spread further light throughout Europe and the World and hopefully to bring more peace. At the same time there was a concern that the upcoming crusades that were definitely happening at this time were going to destroy many Holy relics and sacred texts and other things that were important to the primordial tradition. The order was organized, really, to go out and establish contacts with these other mystical traditions and to secure some of the documents and artifacts within the Holy Land to ensure they wouldn't be destroyed by crusaders or by the Church itself.[4]

Governments and religious leaders have long suspected the Catholic church of holding religious artifacts and documents and keeping their existence or whereabouts silent. One such secret, which they held on to for over seven hundred years, was the fact that they had no evidence to back up the accusations they used to destroy the Knights Templar. In 2001, Italian researcher Barbara Frale discovered a historical document known as the Chinon Parchment in the Vatican secret archives. In the document, Frale found that in 1308 Pope Clement V had absolved the leaders of the Knights Templar from the accusations they were charged with. Frale was quoted as saying, "I could not believe it when I found it. The paper was put in the wrong archive in the 17th century" and went further to state that "this is proof that the Templars were not heretics, the Pope was obliged to ask pardon from the knights. . . . For 700 years we have believed that the Templars died as cursed men, and this absolves them."[5] The pope's decision, however, did not sit well with King Philip IV of France, so Clement reversed his verdict. The Templar Grand Master Jacques de Molay and others were tortured and burned to death over a slow fire, and the Templars were no more—officially. While burning to death, de Molay is said to have called out to the pope and Philip IV, saying that within a year they would both join him in death. They did. In France and other states throughout Europe, the surviving Templar Knights either went underground or joined rival orders. In other nations, such as Portugal, the Templars were found to be innocent and allowed to carry on under an alternate name, the Knights of Christ.

The Templars were extremely wealthy, and in many respects, they operated much like an international banking corporation would today; they even created a type of traveler's check so that pilgrims traveling to the Holy Land did not have to worry about getting robbed. They received grants of lands, money, and other goods from people, including the king of Aragon, who left them very large tracts of land in

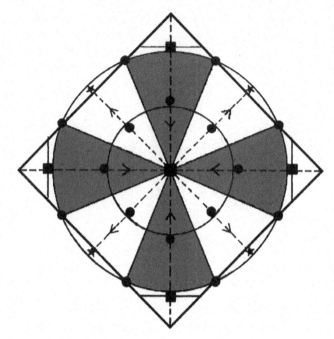

Fig. 10.2. Cross of the Knights Templar
overlaid on the Veil template

Spain. In addition, the king of France, Philip IV, was deeply indebted to them, as were many kingdoms at that time, so when the morning raid came in 1307, the king and the pope were shocked when they found very little in terms of gold and silver. According to *Holy Blood, Holy Grail,* "At dawn on Friday, October 13, 1307, all Templars in France were to be seized and placed under arrest by the king's men, their preceptories placed under sequestration, their goods confiscated. But although Philip's objective of surprise might seem to have been achieved, his primary interest—the order's immense wealth—eluded him. It was never found, and what became of the fabulous 'treasure of the Templars' has remained a mystery."[6]

There are legends that at least some of the treasure was secreted in wagons and hidden away in and around Rennes-le-Château, and in my opinion there seems to be more than enough evidence to support those claims. Other legends have surviving Templars entering

Switzerland and eventually forming the Swiss banking system. The Templars had a fleet of ships in the port at La Rochelle, France, which were reported to be there until just before Philip's dawn raid, when it was discovered they had vanished. Baigent, Leigh, and Lincoln write:

> There is persuasive evidence of some sort of organized flight by a particular group of knights virtually all of whom were in some way connected with the Order's Treasurer. It is not perhaps surprising, therefore, that the treasure of the Temple, together with almost all its documents and records, should have disappeared. Persistent but unsubstantiated rumors speak of the treasure being smuggled by night from the Paris preceptory, shortly before the arrests. According to these rumors, it was transported by wagons to the coast presumably to the Order's naval base at La Rochelle and loaded into eighteen galleys, which were never heard of again. Whether this is true or not, it would seem that the Templars' fleet escaped the king's clutches because there is no report of any of the Order's ships being taken. On the contrary, those ships appear to have vanished totally, along with whatever they might have been carrying.[7]

What were all those ships carrying, and where did they go?

One of the safest places for the Templar ships to flee was Scotland (see fig. 10.3, page 96). At that time, the king of Scotland, Robert the Bruce, had killed a man in church and had been excommunicated by the same pope who condemned the Templars. Because the barons and citizens of Scotland did not rise up against their king, the entire country was excommunicated. What better place for the Templars to flee than to a country that did not care much for the Catholic church or its pope?

This is where the story of Scotland's Rosslyn Chapel, built by William St. Clair (some say Sinclair), and its connection with the Knights Templar usually enters the story. According to George Smart, author of *The Knights Templar Chronology,* "The Sinclair family has

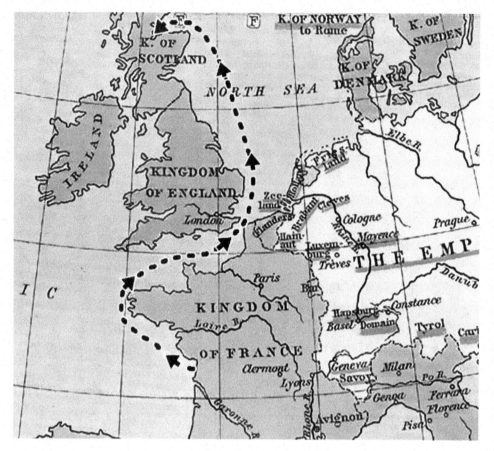

Fig. 10.3. Suspected course of the Templar fleet
in 1307 from France to Scotland

long been associated with the Templars because they were one of the
first families to give land grants to the Templars when they came
back from the Holy Land in the 1120s."[8] In his book *The Square
and Compasses: In Search of Freemasonry,* Freemason Don Falconer
provides us with another link connecting the St. Clair family to
the Templars. Falconer states that "significant in the history of the
Knights Templar is the fact that their first Grand Master, Hugues
de Payen, was married to Catherine de St. Clair. She was a Scottish
woman of Norman descent, who set up the first Templar preceptory
outside the Holy Land on her family's property, a few kilometers

south of Edinburgh. This was the Preceptory of Balantrodoch, in the village now called Temple, not far from where Rosslyn Chapel was built later."[9] Falconer further informs us that "Rosslyn Chapel also has a scroll shrine in the form of a vault sealed under a meter of rock, the contents of which are unknown, but which authors Christopher Knight and Robert Lomas believe may contain relics from the vaults under the Temple at Jerusalem."[10] Some of the more mysterious symbols in Rosslyn Chapel have been identified as depicting plant life that is only found in North America, which is very mysterious, as the chapel was constructed more than two decades before Christopher Columbus arrived in the New World. Falconer writes:

> This gives weight to the belief that, after its arrival in Scotland, the Templar fleet sailed west in search of the land that is called Merica in the Nasorean scrolls and marked by a star. It seems that the Templars almost certainly landed on the New England coast of America early in 1308, and after settling there journeyed back to Scotland more than once. This contention is supported by the famous image of a fourteenth century knight carved on a rock at Westford in Massachusetts and also by the stone tower at Newport in Rhode Island, constructed like a round Templar church, that was referred to as an existing "Norman Villa" by the Italian navigator Giovanni de Verrazano, who was thought to be the first European to discover that part of the coastline.[11]

Jim Egan, author and curator of the Newport Tower Museum in Newport's Touro Park, has laid out a convincing case that the Newport Tower was constructed by John Dee and used as a camera obscura to track alignments of the sun and moon (see fig. 10.4, page 98). As Hogan points out, whether the Newport Tower was built by John Dee or the Knights Templar, "both theories lead to the same source" because Dee was clearly in a line of succession leading back to the Knights Templar.

When speaking of these subjects, you can't avoid discussing

Fig. 10.4. The old stone tower in Touro Park, Newport,
Rhode Island, circa 1894

what many believe is the location of the Holy Grail, the Ark of the
Covenant, ancient records, and potentially massive amounts of treasure. That location is referred to as the Money Pit, aka the Oak Island
Treasure, in Nova Scotia. The legend of the Oak Island Treasure
goes back over two hundred years, when three teenage boys located a
depression in the earth. It was beneath an oak limb that is said to have
borne evidence that a block and tackle had been used on it, allegedly
for the purpose of lowering something heavy into a hole. With images

of treasure in their minds, the boys began digging, and every ten feet they would find timbers and stones. They continued digging, and it just kept going. Every ten feet, they found the same thing: timbers and stones laid out in such a way as to suggest that they were put there by man. They eventually gave up, but the legend grew, and since that time numerous people, including the famous actor and Freemason John Wayne and even President Franklin Delano Roosevelt, have tried to recover the alleged treasure. To date, no known treasure has been recovered from the site, and six men have lost their lives searching for it.

Fig. 10.5. Franklin D. Roosevelt (third from right) and others at Oak Island, Nova Scotia

The Knights Templar and their connections with the St. Clair family; Rosslyn Chapel, with its numerous symbols suggesting the discovery of the New World at least two decades before Columbus; Newport Tower; Oak Island in Nova Scotia, not to mention the alleged treasure buried there—these are all very tantalizing pieces in the puzzle. There is however, one additional connection, which ties in with the Veil and Tree of Life templates, Nicolas Poussin, Rosslyn Chapel, and more. This story is no less amazing and provides more evidence that the locations indicated by the Veil template were known about prior to the founding of the United States.

11   THE STONE OF FOUNDATION

*And Jacob went out from Beersheba, and went toward
Haran. And he lighted upon a certain place, and tarried
there all night, because the sun was set, and he took of the
stones of that place, and put them for his pillows, and lay
down in that place to sleep. And he dreamed, and behold
a ladder set up on the earth, and the top of it reached
to heaven and behold the angels of God ascending and
descending on it.*

GENESIS 28:10–12

On March 17, 2006, a press conference was held at Shugborough
Hall, Lichfield Estate, Staffordshire, England, regarding the enig-
matic Shepherd's Monument and the codes and ciphers it contains.
The general manager of Shugborough Hall, Richard Kemp, introduced
the internationally renowned cryptologist Louis Buff Parry, who had
assisted authorities with investigations regarding the 9/11 attacks and
the downing of Pan Am flight 103. Parry was there that day to reveal
his beliefs regarding the codes and ciphers embedded in the Shepherd's
Monument, which he seems to have solved. In his presentation,
Parry explained how in 1743, members of the La Vérendrye scouting

expedition removed a stone tablet from a natural sandstone pillar in what is now southern Alberta, Canada, and that on another sandstone pillar nearby, the word *PRESTON* was carved in Hebrew letters. Parry added that approximately twenty-eight years earlier, the stone may have been in Scotland at Rosslyn Chapel in 1715 when "the Jacobites took this stone from Rosslyn Chapel niche and marched behind it to Preston, where their campaign was temporarily quashed."[1] Parry explained that Ralph Standish, one of the members of the Jacobite uprising, had his properties seized and went into exile to New England, which is partially verified in an 1841 article in *Bradshaw's Manchester Journal,* which states, "In 1715 we find that Ralph Standish, the son of William Standish and Cecily, the sole heir of the second Sir Robert Blindloss, was engaged in the unfortunate affair at Preston, when the estate was seized by government, but his mother being then alive and proving the manor of Borwick to be her own private property, it was restored, and her eldest son, settling here, made great improvements in the house and gardens."[2] Parry went on to state that "the Standish family property and estate which was confiscated in 1715, is the same property that later becomes the property of George Anson, who builds the Lichfield Estate and Shepherd's Monument on it." Parry suggested that the stone that was found in southern Alberta was placed there by Standish and found by the expedition headed by Pierre Gaultier de Varennes, Sieur de la Vérendrye, who handed it over to Jesuits. From there it is said to have been aboard a ship in 1746, part of a French fleet headed by Captain Jacques-Pierre de Taffanel de la Jonquière, who "was returning some weather damaged ships in his fleet from Quebec in Nova Scotia to France. Admiral George Anson captured part of that fleet (on record) and some of its treasure including the inscribed stone tablet. The stone was apparently then reposed by Admiral George Anson at his family's Lichfield Estate and enshrined in memory by way of the Shepherd's Monument in an interlinked set of codes and ciphers."[3] In the course of a TV documentary, Parry, laying out a convincing case, pointed out that the stone in question is, in his belief, the Pillow Stone of the

Fig. 11.1. *Jacob's Dream* by Bartolome Esteban Murillo, 1660–65

biblical Jacob, mentioned in the passage quoted at the beginning of this chapter.

The Pillow Stone of Jacob is attached to numerous legends and has just as many names: the Stone of Scone, which was used in the coronation of Scottish kings for centuries; Lia Fáil, "the stone that roared"; and the Coronation Stone, over which British monarchs have traditionally been crowned. One of the many legends regarding the stone is that the prophet Jeremiah carried it with him to Ireland, from which it eventually made its way to Scotland. This ties it in with the story of Ralph Standish, the Jacobite uprising, Rosslyn Chapel, La Vérendrye, and the Shepherd's Monument at Shugborough Hall.

Another of the many names attributed to the Pillow Stone, often used in Judaism and Freemasonry, is the Stone of Foundation. While in Freemasonry the stone is viewed purely in a mythical and allegorical light and is not to be confused with other symbolic stones, such as the cornerstone, keystone, or rough ashlar, the Freemasons have over the centuries done a great job of extracting the most logical narratives from all the legends regarding the stone. In *The Symbolism of Freemasonry,* Albert Gallatin Mackey writes:

> We find in the third chapter of the *"Treatise on the Temple"* written by the celebrated Maimonides, the following narrative—"There was a stone in the Holy of Holies, on its west side, on which was placed the Ark of the Covenant, and before it the pot of manna and Aaron's rod. But when Solomon had built the temple, and foresaw that it was, at some future time, to be destroyed, he constructed a deep and winding vault underground, for the purpose of concealing the ark, wherein Josiah afterwards, as we learn in the Second Book of Chronicles, deposited it, with the pot of manna, the rod of Aaron, and the oil of anointing." The Talmudical book "Yoma" gives the same tradition, and says that "the Ark of the Covenant was placed in the center of the Holy of Holies, upon a stone rising three fingers' breadth above the floor, to be, as it were, a pedestal for it." "This stone," says Prideaux, "the Rabbins call the Stone of Foundation."[4]

Of the many names attributed to it, the Stone of Foundation in particular, and the legends and history behind it, suggests possibilities I would never have dreamed of, which coincide with the symbolism of the Veil template. Symbols can be used to describe just about anything, but certain ones, such as numbers, can in many cases serve as signatures. The Stone of Foundation is an important symbol in Freemasonry as well as in other societies and religions, so their views or beliefs about it can be useful in determining whether you're heading in the right direction. The author of the website titled "From Pentagram to Pyramids, Masonic and Kabbalistic Symbols in the Washington, DC Map" states that the emblem of the Stone of Foundation is created by bisecting the sides of a square twice and then bisecting the corners of the square, giving us a square divided into eight sections, as shown in figure 11.2 at left. On the right image of figure 11.2, I've lightened the main lines on the template. I say those are the main lines because they are the lines that fall in line with the adjoining cells making up the entire Veil template.

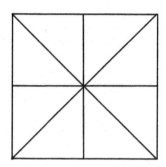 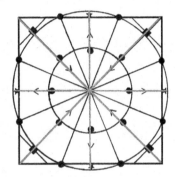

Fig. 11.2. The Stone of Foundation (left) compared with a single cell of the Veil template (right)

Mackey says that the Ark of the Covenant rested on the Stone of Foundation, which is said to bear the inscription of the Tetragrammaton YHWH (יהוה), the sacred four-letter name of God. The Divine Presence of God dwelled over the Ark of the Covenant. The Stone of Foundation, being located between the Earth and the Divine, is symbolic of the joining of Heaven and Earth, signified by the square (Earth) and the circle (Heaven) in the template. The Masonic symbol for the Stone of Foundation, divided into eight sections, resonates with the shape of an octagon, which in turn calls to mind the squaring of a circle or the joining of Heaven and Earth, and that takes us back to the layout of the Dome of the Rock.

Another symbolic reference to the joining of Heaven and Earth, as well as to Freemasonry, can be found in the sixteen lines inside the inner circle and outer circle of the Veil template, as well as the two rough circles found within the shape of the Dome of the Rock.

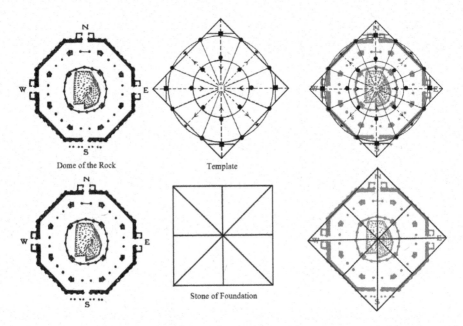

Fig. 11.3. Top row: Dome of the Rock (left), single cell of the Veil template
(center), and Dome of the Rock with Veil template overlay (right).
Bottom row: Dome of the Rock (left), the Stone of
Foundation (center), and Dome of the Rock
with Stone of Foundation overlay (right).

Two circles, each divided into 16 lines, can be viewed as 32 lines
(2 × 16 = 32). The 10 sefiroth and 22 paths in the Tree of Life add
up to 32, and the Tree of Life also symbolizes the connection between
Earth and Heaven. There are 32 degrees in Scottish Rite Freemasonry,
which also uses the double-headed eagle as a symbol, and as we saw
earlier, the double-headed eagle is symbolic of the Tree of Life. In that
light, the Stone of Foundation, its symbolic representation as illus-
trated in figure 11.3, and both the Tree of Life and Veil templates can
be viewed as representing the same concept.

It seemed to fit nicely until it dawned on me that the Stone of
Foundation is in the center of the Dome of the Rock and that Mackey
stated it was the breadth of three fingers. The stone wasn't the Dome of
the Rock; it was set between the Ark of the Covenant and the Earth.

If the legends regarding the stone, like that of the stone associated with the Jacobite uprising, are true, the stone couldn't have been too large, as that stone was carried with the Jacobites in their march to Preston, England. That is when it all fell into place. The Dome of the Rock itself is made up of three octagons, clearly visible in the layout (fig. 11.4). Octagons are viewed as the squaring of the circle, much like the Veil template, which consists of a square and a circle, and consists of small, medium, and large templates, as I mentioned in chapter 6.

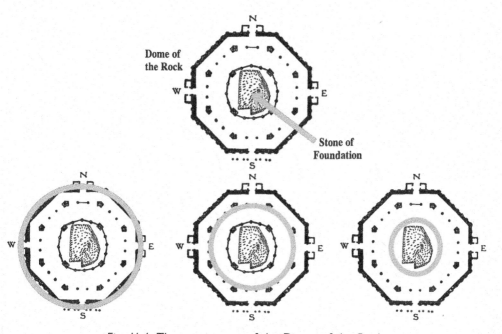

Fig. 11.4. Three octagons of the Dome of the Rock, or the veils of the Stone of Foundation

After years of researching treasure legends, I've often read and heard of smaller treasures used as decoys to hide larger treasures. A veil essentially serves the same purpose—a decoy, hiding the more sacred treasures in the Dome of the Rock. One of those sacred treasures is the Stone of Foundation, which serves as a symbol of the unification of Heaven and Earth, and is veiled by the three octagons that make up the Dome of the Rock, just as the Tree of Life template is veiled by the Veil template, which itself contains concentric circles that form three octagons, or squared circles.

Fig. 11.5. The Three Veils, as represented
by the three concentric circles

12   LOOKING BEHIND THE VEIL

Two symbols in the Veil template had puzzled me from the beginning: the turkey track and the star. There are eight turkey tracks and four star symbols in each cell of the Veil template (fig. 12.1). The turkey track has been the hardest to figure out. While researching, I have found matching symbols in ancient runes, including from the Elder and Younger Futhark, the Celtic, and the Danish, and even in some versions of ancient Phoenician alphabets, which have a symbol that looks identical to the turkey track. Each has a different meaning.

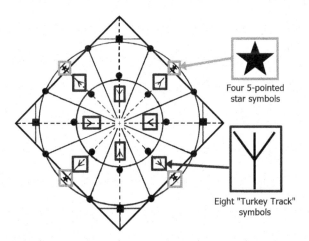

Four 5-pointed
star symbols

Eight "Turkey Track"
symbols

Fig. 12.1. Four star and eight turkey-track symbols on the Veil template

I have also found records of the marks of medieval masons (the cathedral builders) that contain identical symbols. In regard to masons' marks, *Freemason's Quarterly Magazine* of 1853 describes them thus: "True mason's marks are merely the cyphers of operative workmen, to distinguish their own performances."[1] But Robert Freke Gould writes in his 1884 *History of Freemasonry:*

> The marks on both English and French buildings, for the most part, vary in length from 2 to 7 inches, and those found at Cologne from 1½ inch to 2 inches, and were chiefly made . . . to distinguish the work of different individuals. At the present-time the man who works a stone (being different from the man who sets it) makes his mark on the bed or other internal face of it, so that it may be identified. The fact, however, that in the ancient buildings it is only a certain number of the stones which bear symbols—that the marks found in different countries (although the variety is great) are in many cases identical, and in all have a singular accordance in character . . . —seems to show that the men who employed them did so by system, and that the system, if not the same in England, Germany and France, was closely analogous in one country to that of the others. Moreover, . . . many of the signs are evidently religious and symbolical, and agree fully with our notions of the body of men known as the Freemasons.[2]

The Knights Templar, being the wealthiest order of their day, are said to have built at least a thousand churches and other structures throughout Europe and the United Kingdom. In constructing those buildings, they would have needed, and are known to have used, the operative masons. These were the same masons who used symbols that, as Gould observes above, correspond to those of Freemasonry. This is just one more bit of evidence hinting at a connection between the Veil template, the Freemasons, and the Knights Templar.

Figure 12.2, the illustration of masons' marks at Tewkesbury Abbey,

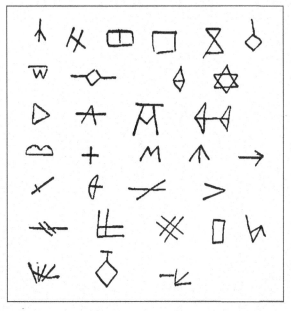

Fig. 12.2. Masons' marks found in Tewkesbury Abbey,
in Gloucestershire, England, including the turkey-track symbol

shows the turkey track at the top left. That same symbol is found in the
crypt at Canterbury Cathedral, the ruins of the Cistercian monastery
known as Fountains Abbey in North Yorkshire, and even in Rosslyn
Chapel in Scotland.[3] What does it mean? I wish I knew. The ambiguous
nature of symbols is part of their beauty, but their ambiguity can also
be frustrating. I've seen other sites suggesting that the symbol could be
translated as the letter M, which is the thirteenth letter of the modern
English alphabet. The equivalent in the Hebrew alphabet is the letter
mem (מ), which is the 13th letter of their alphabet and has a gematria
value of 40.

After noticing the similarities of religious symbols inside Hagia
Sophia, the ancient Greek Orthodox basilica in Istanbul, which served
later as a mosque and currently as a museum, I can't help but wonder
if the turkey tracks could be a crude representation of the symbol we
know as the fleur-de-lis. While we don't have anything definite, we at
least now have a few clues to follow. Also of note is the fish symbol, the

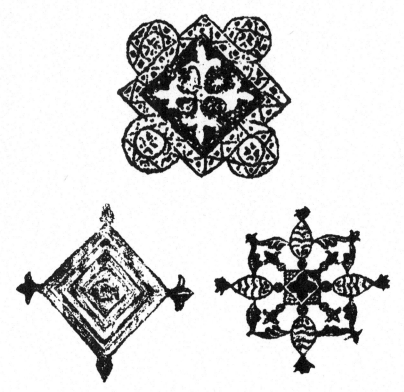

Fig. 12.3. Religious symbols in the ancient Greek Orthodox
basilica Hagia Sophia in Istanbul. Note the similarities of the
symbols above with those of the Veil template.

vesica piscis, and the four stars located on the sides of the symbol at the
top of figure 12.3, which will be discussed later in this chapter.

I found several sources from various authors, all of which explain
how the fleur-de-lis is a representation of the Tree of Life, with origins dating back to ancient Egypt. These authors point out that the
ancient Egyptians used a hieroglyph of a lotus plant, which consists of
3 upright stems, to represent the Tree of Life. This comparison rang a
bell because, as I noted earlier, there are 8 turkey tracks on the template,
each having 4 points, for a total of 32 points, which is equal to the
number of paths in the Kabbalistic Tree of Life. The Egyptian hieroglyph evolved over time and took on the shape of the present, as author
Audrey Fletcher explains:

The ancient Egyptian symbol for *plant* meaning *Tree of Life* was three sacred lotus lilies. They have three stems curving to the left as though blown into life by the breath of Hu, the celestial sphinx. On top of each stem is the Lotus flower which was used in ancient Egypt to represent life and resurrection. It is from this hieroglyph that the "fleur de lis," which is frequently found in ancient Egyptian art traces its origin. The "fleur de lis" represents the Tree of Life. The glyph which denotes the sacred knowledge associated with Hu is also formed by the three stems of the sacred lotus lilies. The Osiris crown can be similary considered in these terms. Following the role model of Osiris, in 1346 AD Edward the Black Prince won three feathers at Crecy which he adopted as his emblem. If the three feathers are gathered at the stems a "fleur de lis" is created.[4]

Fig. 12.4. The ancient Egyptian hieroglyph for the lotus (top) evolved into what we now know as the fleur-de-lis.

I submit that the symbol isn't a turkey track drawn by a member of the Knights of the Golden Circle, but rather a representation of an ancient glyph symbolizing the Tree of Life, most likely drawn by a Freemason or someone of a like mind who came before.

As for the five-pointed star, research has uncovered more than enough to offer an explanation that ties in with the other symbolic meanings involved in the Veil template. As many know, the five-pointed star has long been used as a symbol for the planet Venus, the morning and evening star, and for the mythological goddess (yet another feminine aspect to the Veil template), but there is more. As previously stated, the Veil template is made up of individual cells, which fit together to form the whole veil. In regard to the crisscrossed lines made by the Veil template, Fulcanelli remarks, "It is the child Jesus, carried by Offerus, the servant or the Traveler; it is the gold in its bath, the bather; it is the bean, the sabot, the cradle or the cross of honour and it is also the fish 'which swims in our philosophic water.'"[5] He compares the fish, which swims in the philosophic water, to a hieroglyph of the Philosophers' Stone in its first state. His mention of Jesus and the fish brings up the fish symbol used by early and modern Christians alike.

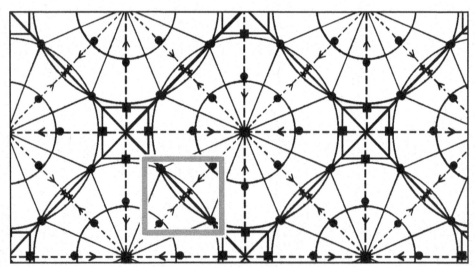

Fig. 12.5. Veil template, highlighting the vesica piscis

The symbol of the fish, which is often used to represent Christianity, is also known as the vesica piscis and is derived from the overlapping of two circles. "The word usually found inscribed within, IXOYE [*sic*] (Ichthus), is Greek, meaning *fish* [see fig. 12.6]. The emblem became significant to Christians after St. Augustine, who extracted the word from the acrostic prophecy of the Erythraean Sibyl, and applied the kabbalistic technique of notarikon (acrostic) to the word to reveal 'Jesus Christ, God's son, savior.'"[6]

Figure 12.7 on page 117 depicts Christ within a vesica piscis, also known as a mandorla, or almond shape. The four evangelists surrounding Christ are depicted as their symbolic creatures: man, ox, lion, and eagle. These four creatures also happen to represent the fixed signs of the zodiac: Aquarius, Taurus, Leo, and Scorpio. (The eagle is sometimes used to represent Scorpio instead of the scorpion.) Also of note are the crisscrossed lines (veil), circles (female), and squares (male) throughout the illustration.

> The custom of the early Christians to communicate by drawing a portion [of the vesica piscis] in the dust was carried over from the practice of the ancient Pythagoreans, who discovered the shape's unique properties and made it an important part of their teachings.

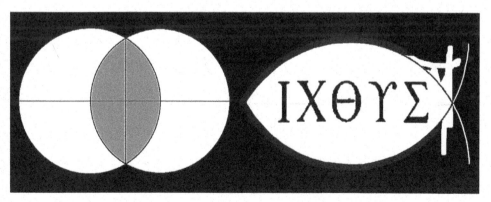

Fig. 12.6. The vesica piscis symbol. The Greek IXΘΥΣ (*ichthus*), meaning *fish*, forms an acrostic for *Iesous Christos, theou huios, soter:* "Jesus Christ, Son of God, Savior."

In earlier times, this glyph was associated with the goddess Venus, and represented female genitalia. Early depictions of Christ depict Him as an infant within the vesica (in this context, it is usually referred to as a mandorla, meaning "almond shaped"), which represented the womb of Mary, and often, the coming together of Heaven and Earth in the body of Jesus (part man, part God). As such, it is also a doorway or portal between worlds, and symbolizes the intersection between the heavens and the material plane.[7]

Just as the symbol of the net or veil can be viewed as dividing the temporal and spiritual worlds, Jesus can be viewed as the coming together of Heaven and Earth, or the portal between man and God. This symbolism carries over to the Stone of Foundation, which is said to have rested between the Ark of the Covenant and the floor in the Holy of Holies. In this light, the symbols of the vesica piscis, the veil, Jesus, the Stone of Foundation, the crisscross patterns of the alchemical process explained by Fulcanelli, and the hieroglyphic symbol of the first stage of the Philosophers' Stone can all be viewed as one.

The Veil template is representative of all the above. The template, with its dimensions, scale, and symbols, can be viewed as representing aspects of Judaism, Christianity, Islam, the Ark of the Covenant, the Stone of Foundation, astronomy, mysticism, Greek mythology, Pythagoreanism, masculine and feminine aspects, the joining of Heaven and Earth, the Dome of the Rock, alchemy, Freemasonry, the Rosicrucians, and beliefs carried down through operative masons (the cathedral builders) as well as the Knights Templar. Many of the symbols attributed to those mentioned above can be traced even further back to cultures like ancient Egypt and Phoenicia. It is amazing to me how one seemingly simple symbol like the Veil template can incorporate such complex and diverse meanings from throughout history. It does a very good job, in my opinion, of drawing a picture of Abraham Abulafia's dream for Christians, Jews, and Muslims to unite through the beliefs they held in common. I believe that was also an idea held

Fig. 12.7. Illuminated image of Christ and the four animal symbols
of the four evangelists from the *Codex Bruchsal*, circa 1220,
Evangelistar von Speyer. Note that Christ is seated in a vesica piscis.

Fig. 12.8. *The Rending of the Veil* by William Bell Scott, 1869

by the founders of the Knights Templar as well as by many within Rosicrucianism and Freemasonry to this day.

The diameter of the outer circle in the large Veil template is 124 miles. The number 124 is the gematria for one of the Hebrew words for *veil* (מעטה). Drawing a line from one star directly across the diameter to the star on the other side of the circle and then back gives us two lines, each one having a length of 124 miles, for a total of 248 miles. The stars on the template are located within the vesica piscis. The distance of 248 miles from one star to the other is also the gematria of the Hebrew word for *womb* (רחם, *rechem*)—248!

Leviticus 16:2 reads, "And the Lord said unto Moses, Speak unto Aaron thy brother, that he come not at all times into the holy place within the vail before the mercy seat, which is upon the ark; that he die not: for I will appear in the cloud upon the mercy seat." *Veil* (*vail* in the archaic spelling of the King James Version) can mean *to hide or conceal,* but it can also be regarded as protecting people from that which is behind it, as in the verse above.

13   RE-VEILING THE MAPS

Many cultures, religions, and societies throughout the world and history alike have legends, symbols, and interpretations regarding veils. In Royal Arch Freemasonry, there is a ceremony known as the "passing of the veils," which, like most Masonic symbols, can have multiple interpretations. This ceremony is said to have changed throughout the years; in some instances, it has been ignored by Freemasons in various countries.

One interpretation is that the veil has alchemical symbolism, which I have covered in chapter 6 of this book regarding Fulcanelli. In a paper titled "Passing the Veils: Ceremony and History" Gordon Mogg observes that "in the early ceremonies, the veils were three in number." Mogg goes on to note that the Kabbalistic text *The Book of the Greater Holy Assembly* refers to the three veils of negative existence.

> The first veil is called in Hebrew, AIN (which means 'No'), i.e., negatively. The name is spelled with three letters and foreshadows the first three sefiroth. The second veil is called AIN SOF, which means "no bound" or "boundless." In Hebrew, this name is written with six letters and it alludes to the first six sefiroth [of the Kabbalistic Tree of Life]. The third veil is called AIN SOF AUR, which means "unbounded light." This name consists of nine letters and refers to

Fig. 13.1. My version of the Template

the nine sefiroth. After this there remains Malkuth ("Kingship"), the tenth sefiroth. The Candidate had to pass through these veils, after which he was said to have attained Malkuth or Kingship; that is to say it was the climax of Freemasonry, as, according to General Charles Rainsford; who represented English Freemasonry in 1784, when consulted by French Masons, he contended that the ritual of Freemasonry was derived from the Kabbalists.[1]

Mogg's association of the Royal Arch Mason ceremony involving the passing of the veils with the sefiroth of the Tree of Life does a great job of explaining the two treasure templates I have been describing throughout this book: the Veil and the Tree of Life. When I found

Mogg's paper, I was ecstatic, as it goes hand in hand with what I have discovered.

Another interesting piece of information regarding the Kabbalistic Tree of Life is a division between the top three sefiroth and the seven lower ones. The top three, Crown, Wisdom, and Understanding, can be viewed as representing the Holy Trinity in an esoteric Christian sense, or, in a more traditional Jewish Kabbalistic view, the realm of the superconscious and the conscious intellect. The lower seven sefiroth are often listed as conscious emotions. These two halves can also be viewed as representing the spiritual world above and the physical world below.

Here, it's not so much the meanings I want to focus on but rather the division of the Tree of Life into two parts with the top three sefiroth separated from the bottom seven. We know of two large treasures, mentioned earlier: one in Victorio Peak and the other near Georgetown, Texas. Many have claimed that Victorio Peak was a part of the legendary Cibola, one of the lost Seven Cities of Gold. If that is the case, would it be too far out of the box to wonder if the seven lower sefiroth could possibly give the locations of the Seven Cities of Gold? In that case, what do the locations of the top three sefiroth lead us to? If the bottom seven represent the physical world, the top three might have something to do with the spiritual world.

Timothy Hogan has mentioned that the Knights Templar were concerned with safeguarding sacred relics and texts involving Jewish, Sufi, Druze, and Christian religious traditions, which they felt were being threatened by not only the crusaders but also the Catholic church itself. Could the three higher sefiroth contain sacred relics and texts related to Judaism, Christianity, and Islam? If so, they may contain ancient texts from other cultures, religions, and mystical traditions as well. Hogan has also stated that the Kabbalistic text the *Zohar* and other holy texts were discovered by Templars in the Holy Land and brought to Jewish communities in Spain, where they were published for the first time. He further states that the *Zohar* was published in the same town by the same printers who published the Grail story *Parzival*.

I was not able to find any proof of that claim, but I did find it interesting, because the man given credit for publishing the *Zohar* is Moses de Leon, a Spanish rabbi. Moses de Leon had close contacts with Joseph Gikatilla, whose *Gates of Light* was later published by Paolo Riccio in Latin as *Portae Lucis*. On the engraving for Riccio's *Portae Lucis*, two illustrations caught my eye. The first is a diagram of the Tree of Life, which differs slightly in shape from the illustration on the book's frontispiece. The Tree of Life on the frontispiece is more elongated or triangular on top, whereas the Tree of Life found within the book resembles the more familiar shape for the Tree of Life (see fig. 13.2, page 124). Normally, this wouldn't pose a problem, but it left me wondering which shape should be used in the Tree of Life template on a map.

The second illustration in *Portae Lucis* that caught my eye and ties in with Hogan's observations is found on the last page of *Portae Lucis*. This illustration appears to be of a knight holding a crescent-shaped object over his head. In the top center of that object is what appears to be a cup, possibly a representation of the Holy Grail (see fig. 13.3, page 124). Why would an illustration of a knight holding a grail be in there? Considering what appears to be a hidden map on the frontispiece along with a hooked X symbol and other symbols, I can't help but wonder if stories of lost Templar treasures and Grail legends are within the realm of possibility.

Displaying the maps has proven to be a little more complicated than I had anticipated, mainly because they cover such large areas. Another problem with displaying locations is the potential for lawsuits brought on by my giving locations, possibly resulting in swarms of people creating a nuisance by descending onto private property in their search for treasure that may or may not be present. I will, however, give locations to areas located on public lands. Just make sure you follow local, state, and federal laws when searching and always gain permission in writing if you decide to search for one or more of these treasures. The locations I will list may or may not contain buried treasure or relics, but using the dimensions I have listed in this book will give you everything you need to locate all the other locations across the continent. As I stated before,

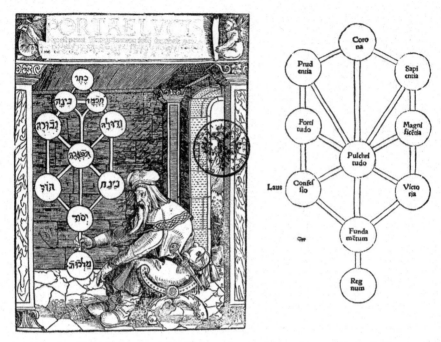

Fig. 13.2. Frontispiece of *Portae Lucis* with its Tree of Life (left) and a similar Tree of Life from within the book (right).

PORTAELVCIS

fimue pertranfeas/quin ſingula cui ex ſacris nominibus ac ſphī
riſtico accomodentur & congruant cœnobio diſcernas:quod ſi
fidens ardenter peregeris;ſublimiũ legis penetraliũ conſors eua
des/ineffabilium dei archanorum particeps efficieris/ eorumcȝ
pſal. 90 aſcriberis numero quibus diuina ſpondent eloquia Roborabo
ipſum quoniam cognouit nomen meum.Huic igitur tanquam
reſerandæ arcis veſtibulo epithomati lȩtus inſiſte;vt quæ deinſ
ceps altiſſimi nutu enodare conabor promptius intuearis.Nos
itaque condignos imperſcrutabilis altaque clementia conſtituat
vt pertinaces expetitæ doctrinæ cultores:& ipſius legis amore
probati executores perſiſtere valeamus:& in nobis demũ quod
yſa. 54 ſcriptum eſt effulgeat. Filij tui edocti deo;& multa filiorum
tuorum pax erit. Amen.

Excuſa in officina Millerana Auguſtæ Vindelicoſ
rũ. quinto Idus Iunias. Anno ſalutis humanȩ
M. D. XVI.

Fig. 13.3. Illustration on the final page of *Portae Lucis*

each cell in the Veil template doesn't contain a treasure; many do, but not all, much as a city map is full of buildings yet there are vacant areas throughout the city. In this case there are many vacancies. If a person knows of a treasure legend in an area, application of the Veil template may help you narrow down any possible locations—that is, if that treasure is connected to any of the groups listed in previous chapters.

Before I reveal the maps, I want to point out an additional sefirah often used in the Kabbalistic Tree of Life: Da'ath or Knowledge. The location of Da'ath on this map is between Lynnville, Kentucky, and Palmersville, Tennessee, very close to the border between the two states. On the map of the Tree of Life template in figure 13.4 below, I have added the location for this additional sefirah and marked it with a dashed circle.

One location on the Veil template that is located on public lands is in Oklahoma and has a treasure story to go along with it. One source claims that Jesse James and his gang hid a large treasure, or at least

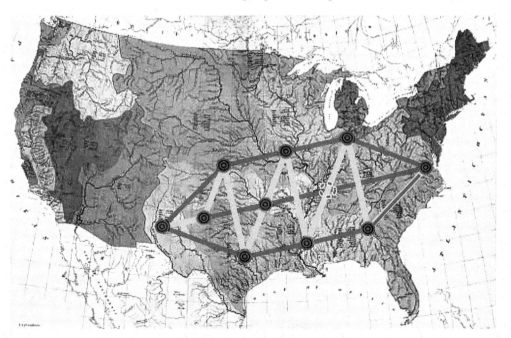

Fig. 13.4. Tree of Life template superimposed
on a map of the United States

a portion of it, on Tarbone Mountain, which is located within the boundaries of the Wichita Mountains National Wildlife Refuge. This particular site is on the small Veil template, and when one is looking at the small template, it would be located on the southwestern star. Another location on this same small Veil template, also located within the confines of the Wichita Mountains National Wildlife Refuge, is approximately 3.4 miles east-southeast of Tarbone Mountain. This location would be the bottom star within the lower corner of the template (fig. 13.5). The center of this small template is located approximately 33.97 degrees and 4.42 miles from the location on Tarbone Mountain. Using this will give you the bearing of the entire Veil template (with the small, medium, and large templates in each cell).

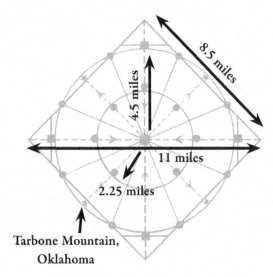

Fig. 13.5. Small template located at
Tarbone Mountain, Oklahoma

Another possible location, in New Mexico, is on a medium-sized Veil template. This site is located inside the boundaries of Petroglyph National Monument on the northwestern side of Albuquerque, New Mexico (fig. 13.6). Based on my map, this potential site is located very near the northernmost parking lot. The center of this medium template is located approximately 247.18 degrees and 18.71 miles from the site at the Petroglyph National Monument.

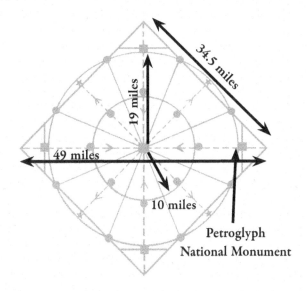

Fig. 13.6 Medium template located at Petroglyph National Monument near Albuquerque, New Mexico

The mention of petroglyphs brings up a curious mystery. This is the Los Lunas Decalogue Stone, which is located near but not within this template. What makes this stone so mysterious are the ancient Hebrew characters carved into it. It is described by author Donald Panther-Yates as "a giant boulder inscribed with the Ten Commandments in Phoenician Hebrew characters. The Indians, Spaniards, and Americans knew of its existence, and the nearby crypto-Jewish community of Los Quelites venerated it, building a secret altar that the Spanish Inquisition smashed and destroyed."[2] The mention of ancient Hebrew carvings in New Mexico reminded me of the Hebrew carving on a sandstone pillar mentioned by Louis Buff Parry in chapter 11 of this book. This sandstone pillar, located hundreds of miles north of New Mexico, is also located at or very near to a location on the Veil template! Was the Decalogue Stone carved by Hebrews or someone who knew the language? Do they, or did they, serve as trail markers to someone in the know? It never ceases to amaze me how the template, when it is laid out over a map, lines up on or very near to known treasure sites and sites of historical importance.

Another potential site located in the center of a large Veil template can be located within Carson National Forest, also in New Mexico. It can be found approximately 188.23 degrees and 9.12 miles south-southwest of the intersection of Highway 434 and North Angel Fire Road in Angel Fire, New Mexico.

I have chosen the sites in Oklahoma and New Mexico chiefly because they are located within public lands. The Veil template covers the entire nation and more, but many of the sites throughout the nation are on private property.

As mentioned in chapter 6, the large, medium, and small templates are all connected. The distances and bearings I have provided give you the angles and distances to piece it all together. As another example of the connection, I've created one more map for you below:

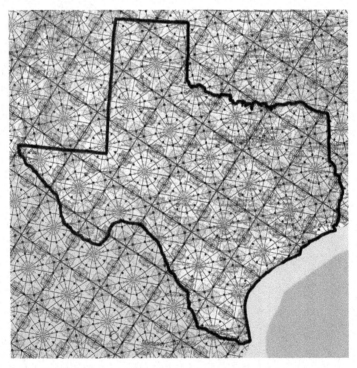

Fig. 13.7. Example of the Veil template placed over a map

I submit that the Tree of Life template gives the locations of two types of treasures. The top three sefiroth, representing Crown, Wisdom, and Understanding, could possibly hold sacred relics and texts dealing with Jewish, Christian, and Islamic religious and mystic beliefs. I wouldn't be shocked if they contain relics and texts dealing with alchemical, occult, and Gnostic traditions as well. The lower seven sefiroth may very well mark the locations of the Seven Cities of Gold.

I believe the Veil template overlays the Tree of Life template, as was explained above in regard to the passing of the veils. I also believe the Veil template contains treasures of various kinds, but I seriously doubt the treasures in the Veil template are of a spiritual nature, like those in the Tree of Life template. As Fulcanelli stated, "The whole work of the art consists in processing this mercury until it receives the above-mentioned sign. And this sign has been called by the ancient authors the *Seal of Hermes, Seal of the Wise (Sel des Sages,* sel, salt, being put instead of Scel, seal, which confuses the mind of seekers), the *Mark* and the *Imprint of the Almighty,* his *Signature,* also the *Star of the Magi, the Pole Star,* etc."[3] A seal serves to cover or protect the more valuable or sacred items within.

The dimensions, scales, symbols, numbers, and their interpretations given in this book hardly seem to give this story the justice it deserves. In some cases, the interpretations are so widely varied that it would take volumes to write about them all. In researching and writing about this topic, I constantly had to catch myself from going off the path and down a rabbit's hole. In fact, I suspect that that is exactly what was intended in some cases, so as to prevent people from getting too close. On the other hand, those who created this beautiful and amazing work may have wanted it to be found, and wanted whoever found it to have to work hard in doing so, knowing full well that the path of discovery would lead the seeker to question himself and everything he previously thought he knew. There is so much more to this story, and so much more that I am sure we have yet to discover.

✪

This journey has been an amazing one, and it is far from over. I started searching for my great-great-grandfather's treasure, which I first imagined as being at most a few jars of gold and silver coins, yet as it turned out, I ended up stumbling over what I truly believe could be one of the biggest treasure stories of all time, spanning over two thousand years. Just thinking of that, along with the history and lives of the people involved, is extremely humbling. I don't believe a person can read something without being affected on some level, and researching the topics involved in this story has changed me profoundly. It has opened my eyes, or lifted a veil from before them, to deeper meanings behind what we perceive as reality, far beyond the everyday static of our ordinary lives. I hope that those who read this will do their own research and possibly expand on the work I have done. I believe if you do, you too will view the knowledge you gain as your own personal and priceless treasure, and, who knows, we may one day meet on this amazing trail of discovery.

NOTES

CHAPTER ONE.
KNIGHTS, OUTLAWS, AND TREASURE MAPS

1. Campbell, "Knights of the Golden Circle."
2. Campbell, "Knights of the Golden Circle."
3. Dawsey and Dawsey, eds., *The Confederados.*
4. Duke, *The Truth about Jesse James, As Told by His Great-Granddaughter Betty Dorsett Duke,* 335.
5. Creavens, "In Local Hospital, 'Jesse James' Scoffs at Treasure Hunters."
6. Duke, *The Truth,* 336.
7. Duke, *The Truth,* 336.

CHAPTER TWO.
SEVEN CITIES OF GOLD

1. Weiser, "Victorio Peak."
2. Abcarian, "Treasure or Treachery?"
3. Taylor, *American Colonies,* vol. 1, 63.
4. Hudnall and Wang, *Spirits of the Border,* 183.
5. Yates, "Cibola."
6. Johnson, "Following 1937 Story of Buried Gold, Family Searches New Mexico's Sands."
7. McCartney, "Victorio Peak's Gold May Never Pan Out but the Saga's One to Treasure."

CHAPTER THREE.
BRUTON PARISH CHURCH

1. "Bruton Parish Church," Colonial Williamsburg website.
2. Dawkins, "The Oak Island Mystery, Part 2: The Navigators."
3. Harold V. B. Voorhis, foreword to Bauer, *Foundations Unearthed.*
4. Voorhis, foreword to Bauer, *Foundations Unearthed.*
5. Rivera, *Mystery at Colonial Williamsburg,* 6.
6. Rivera, *Mystery at Colonial Williamsburg,* 9.
7. Hall, *The Secret Teachings of All Ages,* 542.
8. Haywood, "The Study Club: Chapters of Masonic History."
9. "Wren Building," Colonial Williamsburg website.
10. "Wren Building," Colonial Williamsburg website.
11. Bullock, "Bruton Parish Church (A Restoration)."

CHAPTER FIVE.
SIGNATURES IN NUMBERS

1. Pike, *Morals and Dogma,* 96.
2. Pike, *Morals and Dogma,* 625.
3. Pike, *Morals and Dogma,* 235.
4. Ginsburgh, "Introduction to Gematria."
5. Pike, *Morals and Dogma,* 205.
6. Peters, *Masonic Writings,* 2nd ed., 106.
7. Big Bytes, "A Symbol for Contemplation and Meditation" (site discontinued).
8. Ginsburgh, "The Hebrew Letters: Hei."
9. Ginsburgh, "The Hebrew Letters: Zayin."
10. Ginsburgh, "The Number 18."
11. Clark, "Introduction."

CHAPTER SIX.
THE THREE VEILS

1. Luria, "Elul."
2. Mack, "Botticelli's Venus."
3. Clutterbuck, "History and Antiquities of the County of Hertford," 154.

4. Big Bytes, "Washington DC Monumental Core" (site discontinued).
5. Fulcanelli, *Le mystère des cathédrales*, 149.
6. Big Bytes, "Washington DC Monumental Core" (site discontinued).

CHAPTER SEVEN.
GATES OF LIGHT

1. "Paolo Riccio," Wikipedia, updated March 18, 2018.
2. Kritzler, *Jewish Pirates of the Caribbean*, 29.
3. "Dome of the Rock," Wikipedia, updated Feb. 3, 2017.

CHAPTER EIGHT.
LINE OF SUCCESSION

1. "History and Traditions," College of William & Mary website.
2. Hogan, *Novo Clavis Esoterika*, 25.
3. De Vise, "William and Mary May Be Home to Oldest Standing Schoolhouse for Black Children."
4. "The Ancient and Mystical Order Rosae Crucis," Rosicrucian Order website.
5. Woodward, *Prospero's America*, 33.
6. Mackey, *The History of Freemasonry*, vol. 5, 1136.
7. Baigent, Leigh, and Lincoln, *Holy Blood, Holy Grail*, 66.
8. Deutsch and Mannheimer, "Samson ben Abraham of Sens (RaSHBa or HaRaSH of שאנץ)."
9. Ralls, *The Templars and the Grail*, 38.
10. Hogan, *The Way of the Templar*, 18.

CHAPTER NINE.
ARCADIAN SHEPHERDS

1. "About Us: Peter Dawkins." Francis Bacon Research Trust website.
2. Dawkins, "The Oak Island Mystery, Part 2: The Navigators."
3. Dawkins, "The Oak Island Mystery, Part 3: Swan Secrets."
4. Cassini, *Celestial Globe*. Cassini's globe can also be viewed in 3D detail at Neikirk, "A Sneak Preview of 3D Imaging," Osher Map Library website.

5. Hamblett, "Nicolas Poussin."

6. Ashland, *Ptolemy's Tetrabiblos, or Quadripartite,* 29.

7. "The Summer Triangle, Vega/Lyra," Souled Out website.

8. Pike, *Morals and Dogma,* 818–19.

CHAPTER TEN.
INTO THE SHADOWS

1. Hogan, *The Alchemical Keys to Masonic Ritual,* 9.

2. Hogan, *Novo Clavis Esoterika,* 82.

3. Galley and Verseegen, *Templars' Lost Treasure.*

4. Stone, "Knights Templar, Freemasonry, and Bloodlines of Spiritual Power."

5. Moore, "Vatican Paper Set to Clear Knights Templar."

6. Baigent, Leigh, and Lincoln, *Holy Blood, Holy Grail,* 75.

7. Baigent, Leigh, and Lincoln, *Holy Blood, Holy Grail,* 76.

8. Galley and Verseegen, *Templars' Lost Treasure.*

9. Falconer, *The Square and Compasses.*

10. Falconer, *The Square and Compasses.*

11. Falconer, *The Square and Compasses.*

CHAPTER ELEVEN.
THE STONE OF FOUNDATION

1. Wince, *Lapis Exillis.*

2. Anonymous, "Railway Excursions," 274.

3. Wince, *Lapis Exillis.*

4. Mackey, *The Symbolism of Freemasonry,* 291.

CHAPTER TWELVE.
LOOKING BEHIND THE VEIL

1. "On Symbols and Symbolism," *Freemason's Quarterly Magazine,* 282.

2. Gould, *The History of Freemasonry,* vol. 2, 75–76.

3. Lyndsay, "Rosslyn Chapel."

4. Fletcher, "The Osiris Legend and the Tree of Life: Ancient Egyptians and the Constellations, Part 6."

5. Fulcanelli, *Le mystère des cathédrales,* 149.

6. "Vesica Pisces [*sic*]," SymbolDictionary.net.

7. "Vesica Pisces [*sic*]," SymbolDictionary.net.

CHAPTER THIRTEEN.
RE-VEILING THE MAPS

1. Mogg, "Passing the Veils."

2. Panther-Yates, *Los Lunas Decalogue Stone.*

3. Fulcanelli, *Le mystère des cathédrales,* 149.

BIBLIOGRAPHY

Abcarian, Robin. "Treasure or Treachery? Did 'Doc' Noss Really Find Caverns of Gold or Did He Pull Off a Hoax That Has Plagued His Kin for Years?" *Los Angeles Times,* June 16, 1991.

"About Us: Peter Dawkins." Francis Bacon Research Trust website. Accessed Nov. 29, 2018.

"The Ancient and Mystical Order Rosae Crucis," Rosicrucian Order website. Accessed Nov. 29, 2018.

Anonymous. "Railway Excursions." *Bradshaw's Manchester Journal* 1, no. 18 (Aug. 28, 1841): 274.

Ashland, J. M. *Ptolemy's Tetrabiblos, or Quadripartite: Being Four Books of the Influence of the Stars.* London: Davis and Dickson, 1822.

Baigent, Michael, Richard Leigh, and Henry Lincoln. *Holy Blood, Holy Grail: The Secret History of Christ and the Shocking Legacy of the Grail.* New York: Dell, 2004.

Bauer, Maria. *Foundations Unearthed.* Foreword by Harold V. B. Voorhis. Lancaster, Pa.: Veritas Press, 1948.

Big Bytes. "A Symbol for Contemplation and Meditation: The Tree of Life." Site discontinued.

———. "Washington DC Monumental Core Shown to Be Analogous to the Plan for the Milan Cathedral." Site discontinued.

"Bruton Parish Church." Colonial Williamsburg website. Accessed Nov. 27, 2018.

Bullock, Orin M. "Bruton Parish Church (A Restoration): Architectural Report, Block 21, Building 1, Lot 00." *Colonial Williamsburg Foundation Library*

Research Report, Series 0030. Williamsburg, Va.: Colonial Williamsburg Foundation Library, 1990 [1953]. Accessed Nov. 29, 2018.

Campbell, Randolph B. "Knights of the Golden Circle." Texas State Historical Association website. Accessed Nov. 27, 2018.

Cassini, Giovanni Maria. *Celestial Globe, 1792.* David Rumsey Map Collection website. Accessed Nov. 29, 2018.

Clark, Rawn. "Introduction." A Bardon Companion website. Accessed Nov. 29, 2018.

Clutterbuck, Robert. "The History and Antiquities of the County of Hertford." *The Gentleman's Magazine and Historical Chronicle* XCVII, 1827.

Creavens, Dave. "In Local Hospital, 'Jesse James' Scoffs at Treasure Hunters." *Austin American Statesman,* March 14, 1949.

Crowley, Aleister. *777 and Other Qabalistic Writings of Aleister Crowley.* New York: Samuel Weiser, 1973.

Dawkins, Peter. "The Oak Island Mystery, Part 2: The Navigators." Francis Bacon Research Trust website. Accessed Nov. 28, 2018.

———. "The Oak Island Mystery, Part 3: Swan Secrets." Francis Bacon Research Trust website. Accessed Nov. 29, 2018.

Dawsey, Cyrus B., and James M. Dawsey, eds. *The Confederados: Old South Immigrants in Brazil.* Tuscaloosa: University of Alabama Press, 1995.

De Vise, Daniel. "William and Mary May Be Home to Oldest Standing Schoolhouse for Black Children." *Washington Post,* July 23, 2010.

Deutsch, Gotthard, and S. Mannheimer. "Samson ben Abraham of Sens (RaSHBa or HaRaSH of שאנץ)." Jewish Encyclopedia.com. Accessed Nov. 29, 2018.

"Dome of the Rock." Wikipedia. Updated Feb. 3, 2017.

Duke, Betty Dorsett. *The Truth about Jesse James, as Told by His Great-Granddaughter Betty Dorsett Duke.* Revised edition. Greenwood Village, Colo.: Fiddler's Green Press, 2008.

Emerys, Chevalier. *Revelation of the Holy Grail.* Denver: Timothy Hogan, 2007.

Falconer, Donald H. B. *The Square and Compasses.* Vol. 1, *In Search of Freemasonry.* 1999. Accessed on the Pictou County Masons website on Nov. 29, 2018.

Fletcher, Audrey. "The Osiris Legend and the Tree of Life: Ancient Egyptians and the Constellations, Part 6." Archaeoastonomy website, 1999.

Fulcanelli. *Le mystère des cathédrales.* Translated by Mary Sworder. Albuquerque, N. Mex.: Brotherhood of Life, 2000 [1984].

Galley, David, and Tim Verseegen. *Templars' Lost Treasure*. National Geographic Channel, July 29, 2012.

Ginsburgh, Yitzchak. "The Hebrew Letters: Hei." Gal Einai website. Accessed Nov. 29, 2019.

———. "The Hebrew Letters: Zayin." Gal Einai website. Accessed Nov. 29, 2019.

———. "Introduction to Gematria: Hebrew Numerology." Gal Einai website. Accessed Nov. 29, 2018.

———. "The Number 18." Gal Einai website. Accessed Nov. 29, 2018.

Gould, Robert Freke. *The History of Freemasonry: Its Antiquities, Symbols, Constitutions, Customs, Etc.* Vol. 2. New York: J. C. Yorston, 1884.

Hall, Manly Palmer. *The Secret Teachings of All Ages*. New York: Tarcher Perigee, 2003 [1928].

Hamblett, Sandy. "Nicolas Poussin: Archaeologist? Rosicrucian? Guardian of a Great Secret?" Rhedesium Rennes-le-Château Studies website. Accessed March 7, 2017.

Haywood, H. L. "The Study Club: Chapters of Masonic History." *Builder Magazine* 10, no. 2 (Feb. 1924).

"History and Traditions." College of William & Mary website. Accessed Nov. 29, 2018.

Hogan, Timothy. *The Alchemical Keys to Masonic Ritual*. N.p.: lulu.com, 2007.

———. *Novo Clavis Esoterika*. Denver: Timothy W. Hogan, 2016.

———. *The Way of the Templar*. N.p.: lulu.com, 2015.

Hudnall, Ken, and Connie Wang. *Spirits of the Border: The History and Mystery of Fort Bliss, Texas*. New Lebanon, N.Y.: Omega Press, 2003.

Johnson, Dirk. "Following 1937 Story of Buried Gold, Family Searches New Mexico's Sands." *New York Times*, July 29, 1992.

Kritzler, Edward. *Jewish Pirates of the Caribbean: How a Generation of Swashbuckling Jews Carved Out an Empire in the New World in Their Quest for Treasure, Religious Freedom—and Revenge*. New York: Anchor, 2009.

Luria, Yitzchak. "Elul: Pathway upon the Sea." Baruch Emanuel Erdstein, ed. and trans. Kabbalah Online website. Accessed Nov. 29, 2018.

Lyndsay. "Rosslyn Chapel." Little Miss Mortar website, Jan. 11, 2010.

Mack, Charles R. "Botticelli's Venus: Antique Allusions and Medicean Propaganda." *Explorations in Renaissance Culture* 28, no. 1 (winter 2002).

Mackey, Albert Gallatin. *The History of Freemasonry*. Vol. 5, *History of Christian Knighthood*. New York: Masonic History Co., 1921.

———. *The Symbolism of Freemasonry: Illustrating and Explaining Its Science and Philosophy, Its Legends, Myths, and Symbols.* New York: Clark and Maynard, 1869.

Massé, H. J. L. J. (Henri Jean Louis Joseph). *The Abbey Church of Tewkesbury: With Some Account of the Priory Church of Deerhurst, Gloucestershire.* London: George Bell & Sons, 1901.

McCartney, Scott. "Victorio Peak's Gold May Never Pan Out but the Saga's One to Treasure." *Los Angeles Times,* May 3, 1987.

Mogg, Gordon. "Passing the Veils: Ceremony and History." United Supreme Grand Chapter of Mark and Royal Arch Masons of NSW and the ACT website. Accessed June 23, 2017.

Moore, Malcolm. "Vatican Paper Set to Clear Knights Templar." *Telegraph,* Oct. 5, 2007.

Neikirk, David R. "A Sneak Preview of 3D Imaging at the Osher Map Library and Smith Center for Cartographic Education." Osher Map Library website. Accessed March 21, 2019.

"On Symbols and Symbolism, More Especially on Those of the Most Ancient and Honourable Order of Free and Accepted Masons." *Freemason's Quarterly Magazine* 1 (March 31, 1853): 282.

Ortelius, Abraham, Aegid Diesth, and Humphrey Llwyd. *Theatrum orbis terrarum.* Antwerp, Belgium: Aegid Coppenium Diesth, 1570. Map.

Panther-Yates, Donald. *Los Lunas Decalogue Stone: Eighth-Century Hebrew Monument in New Mexico.* Audiobook. Longmont, Colo.: Panther's Lodge, 2013.

"Paolo Riccio." Wikipedia. Updated March 18, 2018.

Peters, Gregory H. *Masonic Writings.* 2nd ed. Sunyavada Press, 2016.

Pike, Albert. *Morals and Dogma of the Ancient and Accepted Scottish Rite of Freemasonry.* Charleston, S.C.: Supreme Council of the Thirty-Third Degree for the Southern Jurisdiction of the United States, 1871.

Ralls, Karen. *The Templars and the Grail: Knights of the Quest.* Wheaton, Ill.: Quest Books, 2003.

Rivera, David Allen. *Mystery at Colonial Williamsburg: The Truth of Bruton Vault.* Rockville, Md.: Rivera Enterprises, 2014.

Schrader, Del, with Jesse James III. *Jesse James Was One of His Names.* Arcadia, Calif.: Santa Anita Press, 1975.

Stone, Sean. "Knights Templar, Freemasonry, and Bloodlines of Spiritual Power."

Interview with Timothy Hogan. Buzzsaw website. Accessed Nov. 29, 2018.

"The Summer Triangle: Vega/Lyra." Souled Out website. Accessed Nov. 29, 2018.

Taylor, Alan. *American Colonies: The Settling of North America*. Vol. 1. New York: Penguin, 2002.

"Vesica Pisces [*sic*] (Ichthys, Jesus Fish, Mandorla)." SymbolDictionary.net. Accessed Nov. 29, 2018.

Weiser, Kathy. "Victorio Peak: New Mexico Mystery Treasure." Legends of America website. Updated Nov. 2017.

Wince, Gavin, director. *Lapis Exillis: The Stone Is the Grail: An Exploration into the World's Most Secret Societies*. Documentary. UFO TV, June 29, 2009.

Woodward, Walter W. *Prospero's America: John Winthrop Jr., Alchemy, and the Creation of New England Culture, 1606–1676*. Williamsburg, Va.: Omohundro Institute of Early American History and Culture, 2010.

"Wren Building: Oldest Academic Structure in America." Colonial Williamsburg website. Accessed Nov. 29, 2018.

Yates, Bill. "Cibola: The Seven Cities of Gold," Ancient History Encyclopedia website, June 4, 2015.

INDEX

BOOKS OF RELATED INTEREST

Memory Palaces and Masonic Lodges
Esoteric Secrets of the Art of Memory
by Charles B. Jameux

Advanced Civilizations of Prehistoric America
The Lost Kingdoms of the Adena, Hopewell, Mississippians, and Anasazi
by Frank Joseph

The Lost Treasure of the Knights Templar
Solving the Oak Island Mystery
by Steven Sora

First Templar Nation
How Eleven Knights Created a New Country and a Refuge for the Grail
by Freddy Silva

Templar Sanctuaries in North America
Sacred Bloodlines and Secret Treasures
by William F. Mann
Foreword by Scott F. Wolter

The Knights Templar in the New World
How Henry Sinclair Brought the Grail to Acadia
by William F. Mann

The Templars and the Assassins
The Militia of Heaven
by James Wasserman

The Ancient Giants Who Ruled America
The Missing Skeletons and the Great Smithsonian Cover-Up
by Richard J. Dewhurst

INNER TRADITIONS • BEAR & COMPANY
P.O. Box 388
Rochester, VT 05767
1-800-246-8648
www.InnerTraditions.com

Or contact your local bookseller